Pages From An Old Volume Of Life

A Collection Of Essays, 1857-1881

by

Oliver Wendell Holmes

Pages From An Old Volume Of Life
A Collection Of Essays, 1857-1881
by Oliver Wendell Holmes

ISBN: 978-93-64283-26-7

Published by

DOUBLE 9 BOOKS

2/13-B, Ansari Road
Daryaganj, New Delhi – 110002
info@double9books.com
www.double9books.com
Tel. 011-40042856

ABOUT THE AUTHOR

Oliver Wendell Holmes Sr. (1809-1894) was a prominent American physician, poet, essayist, and professor, widely recognized for his contributions to literature and medicine. He was a key figure in the American literary scene of the 19th century and is remembered for his wit, wisdom, and innovative writing. • Some of his notable works include: **"The Last Leaf"** **(1831):** A collection of poems that established him as a significant literary figure. **"The Poet at the Breakfast Table"** (1872): A series of reflections and conversations that showcase his wit and philosophical insights. **"The Chambered Nautilus"** (1858): A poem reflecting on the themes of growth and spirituality. Holmes was a leading figure in American literature and a prominent member of the Boston Brahmins, a group of influential and educated families in Boston. His work reflects a deep engagement with both contemporary social issues and timeless philosophical questions. Oliver Wendell Holmes Sr.'s blend of intellectualism and wit made him a beloved figure in American letters. His works continue to be appreciated for their insight into human nature, societal issues, and the philosophical musings of the 19th century. His influence extended beyond literature into the realms of medicine and education, leaving a lasting legacy in multiple fields.

CONTENTS

BREAD AND THE NEWSPAPER

(September, 1861)

This is the new version of the Panem et Circenses of the Roman populace. It is our ultimatum, as that was theirs. They must have something to eat, and the circus-shows to look at. We must have something to eat, and the papers to read.

Everything else we can give up. If we are rich, we can lay down our carriages, stay away from Newport or Saratoga, and adjourn the trip to Europe sine die. If we live in a small way, there are at least new dresses and bonnets and every-day luxuries which we can dispense with. If the young Zouave of the family looks smart in his new uniform, its respectable head is content, though he himself grow seedy as a caraway-umbel late in the season. He will cheerfully calm the perturbed nap of his old beaver by patient brushing in place of buying a new one, if only the Lieutenant's jaunty cap is what it should be. We all take a pride in sharing the epidemic economy of the time. Only bread and the newspaper we must have, whatever else we do without.

How this war is simplifying our mode of being! We live on our emotions, as the sick man is said in the common speech to be nourished by his fever. Our ordinary mental food has become distasteful, and what would have been intellectual luxuries at other times, are now absolutely repulsive.

All this change in our manner of existence implies that we have experienced some very profound impression, which will sooner or later betray itself in permanent effects on the minds and bodies of many among us. We cannot forget Corvisart's observation of the frequency with which diseases of the heart were noticed as the consequence of the terrible emotions produced by the scenes of the great French Revolution. Laennec tells the story of a convent, of which he was the medical director, where all the nuns were subjected to the severest penances and schooled in the most painful doctrines. They all became consumptive soon after their entrance, so that, in the course of his ten years' attendance, all the inmates died out two or three times, and were replaced by new ones. He does not hesitate to attribute the disease from which they suffered to those depressing moral influences to which they were subjected.

So far we have noticed little more than disturbances of the nervous system as a consequence of the war excitement in non-combatants. Take the first trifling example which comes to our recollection. A sad disaster to the Federal army was told the other day in the presence of two gentlemen and a lady. Both the gentlemen complained of a sudden feeling at the epigastrium, or, less learnedly, the pit of the stomach, changed color, and confessed to a slight tremor about the knees. The lady had a "grande revolution," as French patients say,—went home, and kept her bed for the rest of the day. Perhaps the reader may smile at the mention of such trivial indispositions, but in more sensitive natures death itself follows in some cases from no more serious cause. An old gentleman fell senseless in fatal apoplexy, on hearing of Napoleon's return from Elba. One of our early friends, who recently died of the same complaint, was thought to have had his attack mainly in consequence of the excitements of the time.

We all know what the war fever is in our young men,—what a devouring passion it becomes in those whom it assails. Patriotism is the fire of it, no doubt, but this is fed with fuel of all sorts. The love of adventure, the contagion of example, the fear of losing the chance of participating in the great events of the time, the desire of personal distinction, all help to produce those singular transformations which we often witness, turning the most peaceful of our youth into the most ardent of our soldiers. But something of the same fever in a different form reaches a good many non-combatants, who have no thought of losing a drop of precious blood belonging to themselves or their families. Some of the symptoms we shall mention are almost universal; they are as plain in the people we meet everywhere as the marks of an influenza, when that is prevailing.

The first is a nervous restlessness of a very peculiar character. Men cannot think, or write, or attend to their ordinary business. They stroll up and down the streets, or saunter out upon the public places. We confessed to an illustrious author that we laid down the volume of his work which we were reading when the war broke out. It was as interesting as a romance, but the romance of the past grew pale before the red light of the terrible present. Meeting the same author not long afterwards, he confessed that he had laid down his pen at the same time that we had closed his book. He could not write about the sixteenth century any more than we could read about it, while the nineteenth was in the very agony and bloody sweat of its great sacrifice.

Another most eminent scholar told us in all simplicity that he had fallen into such a state that he would read the same telegraphic dispatches over and over again in different papers, as if they were new, until he felt as if he were an idiot. Who did not do just the same thing, and does not often do it still, now that the first flush of the fever is over? Another person always goes through the side streets on his way for the noon extra,—he is so afraid somebody will meet him and tell the news he wishes to read, first on the bulletin-board, and then in the great capitals and leaded type of the newspaper.

When any startling piece of war-news comes, it keeps repeating itself in our minds in spite of all we can do. The same trains of thought go tramping round in circle through the brain, like the supernumeraries that make up the grand army of a stage-show. Now, if a thought goes round through the brain a thousand times in a day, it will have worn as deep a track as one which has passed through it once a week for twenty years. This accounts for the ages we seem to have lived since the twelfth of April last, and, to state it more generally, for that ex post facto operation of a great calamity, or any very powerful impression, which we once illustrated by the image of a stain spreading backwards from the leaf of life open before as through all those which we have already turned.

Blessed are those who can sleep quietly in times like these! Yet, not wholly blessed, either; for what is more painful than the awaking from peaceful unconsciousness to a sense that there is something wrong, we cannot at first think what,—and then groping our way about through the twilight of our thoughts until we come full upon the misery, which, like some evil bird, seemed to have flown away, but which sits waiting for us on its perch by our pillow in the gray of the morning?

The converse of this is perhaps still more painful. Many have the feeling in their waking hours that the trouble they are aching with is, after all, only a dream,—if they will rub their eyes briskly enough and shake themselves, they will awake out of it, and find all their supposed grief is unreal. This attempt to cajole ourselves out of an ugly fact always reminds us of those unhappy flies who have been indulging in the dangerous sweets of the paper prepared for their especial use.

Watch one of them. He does not feel quite well,—at least, he suspects himself of indisposition. Nothing serious,—let us just rub our fore-feet together, as the enormous creature who provides for us rubs his hands, and all will be right. He rubs them with that peculiar twisting movement of his, and pauses for the effect. No! all is not quite right yet. Ah! it is our head that is not set on just as it ought to be. Let us settle that where it should be, and then we shall certainly be in good trim again. So he pulls his head about as an old lady adjusts her cap, and passes his fore-paw over it like a kitten washing herself. Poor fellow! It is not a fancy, but a fact, that he has to deal with. If he could read the letters at the head of the sheet, he would see they were Fly-Paper.—So with us, when, in our waking misery, we try to think we dream! Perhaps very young persons may not understand this; as we grow older, our waking and dreaming life run more and more into each other.

Another symptom of our excited condition is seen in the breaking up of old habits. The newspaper is as imperious as a Russian Ukase; it will be had, and it will be read. To this all else must give place. If we must go out at unusual hours to get it, we shall go, in spite of after-dinner nap or evening somnolence. If it finds us in company, it will not stand on ceremony, but cuts short the compliment and the story by the divine right of its telegraphic dispatches.

War is a very old story, but it is a new one to this generation of Americans. Our own nearest relation in the ascending line remembers the Revolution well. How should she forget it? Did she not lose her doll, which was left behind, when she was carried out of Boston, about that time growing uncomfortable by reason of cannon-balls dropping in from the neighboring heights at all hours,—in token of which see the tower of Brattle Street Church at this very day? War in her memory means '76. As for the brush of 1812, "we did not think much about that"; and everybody knows that the Mexican business did not concern us much, except in its political relations. No! war is a new thing to all of us who are not in the last quarter of their century. We are learning many strange matters from our fresh experience. And besides, there are new conditions of existence which make war as it is with us very different from war as it has been.

The first and obvious difference consists in the fact that the whole nation is now penetrated by the ramifications of a network of iron nerves which flash sensation and volition backward and forward to and from towns and provinces as if they were organs and limbs of a single living body. The second is the vast system of iron muscles which, as it were, move the limbs of the mighty organism one upon another. What was the railroad-force which put the Sixth Regiment in Baltimore on the 19th of April but a contraction and extension of the arm of Massachusetts with a clenched fist full of bayonets at the end of it?

This perpetual intercommunication, joined to the power of instantaneous action, keeps us always alive with excitement. It is not a breathless courier who comes back with the report from an army we have lost sight of for a month, nor a single bulletin which tells us all we are to know for a week of some great engagement, but almost hourly paragraphs, laden with truth or falsehood as the case may be, making us restless always for the last fact or rumor they are telling. And so of the movements of our armies. To-night the stout lumbermen of Maine are encamped under their own fragrant pines. In a score or two of hours they are among the tobacco-fields and the slave-pens of Virginia. The war passion burned like scattered coals of fire in the households of Revolutionary times; now it rushes all through the land like a flame over the prairie. And this instant diffusion of every fact and feeling produces another singular effect in the equalizing and steadying of public opinion. We may not be able to see a month ahead of us; but as to what has passed a week afterwards it is as thoroughly talked out and judged as it would have been in a whole season before our national nervous system was organized.

> *"As the wild tempest wakes the slumbering sea,*
>
> *Thou only teachest all that man can be!"*

We indulged in the above apostrophe to War in a Phi Beta Kappa poem of long ago, which we liked better before we read Mr. Cutler's beautiful prolonged lyric delivered at the recent anniversary of that Society.

Oftentimes, in paroxysms of peace and good-will towards all mankind, we have felt twinges of conscience about the passage,—especially when one of our orators showed us that a ship of war costs as much to build and keep as a college, and that every port-hole we could stop would give us a new professor. Now we begin to think that there was some meaning in our poor couplet. War has taught us, as nothing else could, what we can be and are. It has exalted our manhood and our womanhood, and driven us all back upon our substantial human qualities, for a long time more or less kept out of sight by the spirit of commerce, the love of art, science, or literature, or other qualities not belonging to all of us as men and women.

It is at this very moment doing more to melt away the petty social distinctions which keep generous souls apart from each other, than the preaching of the Beloved Disciple himself would do. We are finding out that not only "patriotism is eloquence," but that heroism is gentility. All ranks are wonderfully equalized under the fire of a masked battery. The plain artisan or the rough fireman, who faces the lead and iron like a man, is the truest representative we can show of the heroes of Crecy and Agincourt. And if one of our fine gentlemen puts off his straw-colored kids and stands by the other, shoulder to shoulder, or leads him on to the attack, he is as honorable in our eyes and in theirs as if he were ill-dressed and his hands were soiled with labor.

Even our poor "Brahmins,"—whom a critic in ground-glass spectacles (the same who grasps his statistics by the blade and strikes at his supposed antagonist with the handle) oddly confounds with the "bloated aristocracy;" whereas they are very commonly pallid, undervitalized, shy, sensitive creatures, whose only birthright is an aptitude for learning,—even these poor New England Brahmins of ours, subvirates of an organizable base as they often are, count as full men, if their courage is big enough for the uniform which hangs so loosely about their slender figures.

A young man was drowned not very long ago in the river running under our windows. A few days afterwards a field piece was dragged to the water's edge, and fired many times over the river. We asked a bystander, who looked like a fisherman, what that was for. It was to "break the gall," he said, and so bring the drowned person to the surface. A strange physiological fancy and a very odd non sequitur; but that is not our present point. A good many extraordinary objects do really come to the surface when the great guns of war shake the waters, as when they roared over Charleston harbor.

Treason came up, hideous, fit only to be huddled into its dishonorable grave. But the wrecks of precious virtues, which had been covered with the waves of prosperity, came up also. And all sorts of unexpected and unheard-of things, which had lain unseen during our national life of fourscore years, came up and are coming up daily, shaken from their bed by the concussions of the artillery bellowing around us.

It is a shame to own it, but there were persons otherwise respectable not unwilling to say that they believed the old valor of Revolutionary times had died out from among us. They talked about our own Northern people as the English in the last centuries used to talk about the French,—Goldsmith's old soldier, it may be remembered, called one Englishman good for five of them. As Napoleon spoke of the English, again, as a nation of shopkeepers, so these persons affected to consider the multitude of their countrymen as unwarlike artisans,—forgetting that Paul Revere taught himself the value of liberty in working upon gold, and Nathaniel Greene fitted himself to shape armies in the labor of forging iron. These persons have learned better now. The bravery of our free working-people was overlaid, but not smothered; sunken, but not drowned. The hands which had been busy conquering the elements had only to change their weapons and their adversaries, and they were as ready to conquer the masses of living force opposed to them as they had been to build towns, to dam rivers, to hunt whales, to harvest ice, to hammer brute matter into every shape civilization can ask for.

Another great fact came to the surface, and is coming up every day in new shapes, — that we are one people. It is easy to say that a man is a man in Maine or Minnesota, but not so easy to feel it, all through our bones and marrow. The camp is deprovincializing us very fast. Brave Winthrop, marching with the city elegants, seems to have been a little startled to find how wonderfully human were the hard-handed men of the Eighth Massachusetts. It takes all the nonsense out of everybody, or ought to do it, to see how fairly the real manhood of a country is distributed over its surface. And then, just as we are beginning to think our own soil has a monopoly of heroes as well as of cotton, up turns a regiment of gallant Irishmen, like the Sixty-ninth, to show us that continental provincialism is as bad as that of Coos County, New Hampshire, or of Broadway, New York.

Here, too, side by side in the same great camp, are half a dozen chaplains, representing half a dozen modes of religious belief. When the masked battery opens, does the "Baptist" Lieutenant believe in his heart that God takes better care of him than of his "Congregationalist" Colonel? Does any man really suppose, that, of a score of noble young fellows who have just laid down their lives for their country, the Homoousians are received to the mansions of bliss, and the Homoousians translated from the battle-field to the abodes of everlasting woe? War not only teaches what man can be, but it teaches also what he must not be. He must not be a bigot and a fool in the presence of that day of judgment proclaimed by the trumpet which calls to battle, and where a man should have but two thoughts: to do his duty, and trust his Maker. Let our brave dead come back from the fields where they have fallen for law and liberty, and if you will follow them to their graves, you will find out what the Broad Church means; the narrow church is sparing of its exclusive formulae over the coffins wrapped in the flag which the fallen heroes had defended! Very little comparatively do we hear at such times of the dogmas on which men differ; very much of the faith and trust in which all sincere Christians can agree. It is a noble lesson, and nothing less noisy than the voice of cannon can teach it so that it shall be heard over all the angry cries of theological disputants.

Now, too, we have a chance to test the sagacity of our friends, and to get at their principles of judgment. Perhaps most, of us, will agree that our faith in domestic prophets has been diminished by the experience of the last six months. We had the notable predictions attributed to the Secretary of State, which so unpleasantly refused to fulfil themselves. We were infested at one time with a set of ominous-looking seers, who shook their heads and muttered obscurely about some mighty preparations that were making to substitute the rule of the minority for that of the majority. Organizations were darkly hinted at; some thought our armories would be seized; and there are not wanting ancient women in the neighboring University town who consider that the country was saved by the intrepid band of students who stood guard, night after night, over the G. R. cannon and the pile of balls in the Cambridge Arsenal.

As a general rule, it is safe to say that the best prophecies are those which the sages remember after the event prophesied of has come to pass, and remind us that they have made long ago. Those who, are rash enough to predict publicly beforehand commonly give us what they hope, or what they fear, or some conclusion from an abstraction of their own, or some guess founded on private information not half so good as what everybody gets who reads the papers,—never by any possibility a word that we can depend on, simply because there are cobwebs of contingency between every to-day and to-morrow that no field-glass can penetrate when fifty of them lie woven one over another. Prophesy as much as you like, but always hedge. Say that you think the rebels are weaker than is commonly supposed, but, on the other hand, that they may prove to be even stronger than is anticipated. Say what you like,—only don't be too peremptory and dogmatic; we know that wiser men than you have been notoriously deceived in their predictions in this very matter.

Ibis et redibis nunquam in bello peribis.

Let that be your model; and remember, on peril of your reputation as a prophet, not to put a stop before or after the nunquam.

There are two or three facts connected with time, besides that already referred to, which strike us very forcibly in their relation to the great events passing around us. We spoke of the long period seeming to have elapsed since this war began. The buds were then swelling which held the leaves that are still green. It seems as old as Time himself. We cannot fail to observe how the mind brings together the scenes of to-day and those of the old Revolution. We shut up eighty years into each other like the joints of a pocket-telescope. When the young men from Middlesex dropped in Baltimore the other day, it seemed to bring Lexington and the other Nineteenth of April close to us. War has always been the mint in which the world's history has been coined, and now every day or week or month has a new medal for us. It was Warren that the first impression bore in the last great coinage; if it is Ellsworth now, the new face hardly seems fresher than the old. All battle-fields are alike in their main features. The young fellows who fell in our earlier struggle seemed like old men to us until within these few months; now we remember they were like these fiery youth we are cheering as they go to the fight; it seems as if the grass of our bloody hillside was crimsoned but yesterday, and the cannon-ball imbedded in the church-tower would feel warm, if we laid our hand upon it.

Nay, in this our quickened life we feel that all the battles from earliest time to our own day, where Right and Wrong have grappled, are but one great battle, varied with brief pauses or hasty bivouacs upon the field of conflict. The issues seem to vary, but it is always a right against a claim, and, however the struggle of the hour may go, a movement onward of the campaign, which uses defeat as well as victory to serve its mighty ends. The very implements of our warfare change less than we think. Our bullets and cannonballs have lengthened into bolts like those which whistled out of old arbalests. Our soldiers fight with weapons, such as are pictured on the walls of Theban tombs, wearing a newly invented head-gear as old as the days of the Pyramids.

Whatever miseries this war brings upon us, it is making us wiser, and, we trust, better. Wiser, for we are learning our weakness, our narrowness, our selfishness, our ignorance, in lessons of sorrow and shame. Better, because all that is noble in men and women is demanded by the time, and our people are rising to the standard the time calls for. For this is the question the hour is putting to each of us: Are you ready, if need be, to sacrifice all that you have and hope for in this world, that the generations to follow you may inherit a whole country whose natural condition shall be peace, and not a broken province which must live under the perpetual threat, if not in the constant presence, of war and all that war brings with it? If we are all ready for this sacrifice, battles may be lost, but the campaign and its grand object must be won.

Heaven is very kind in its way of putting questions to mortals. We are not abruptly asked to give up all that we most care for, in view of the momentous issues before us. Perhaps we shall never be asked to give up all, but we have already been called upon to part with much that is dear to us, and should be ready to yield the rest as it is called for. The time may come when even the cheap public print shall be a burden our means cannot support, and we can only listen in the square that was once the marketplace to the voices of those who proclaim defeat or victory. Then there will be only our daily food left. When we have nothing to read and nothing to eat, it will be a favorable moment to offer a compromise. At present we have all that nature absolutely demands,—we can live on bread and the newspaper.

MY HUNT AFTER "THE CAPTAIN"

In the dead of the night which closed upon the bloody field of Antietam, my household was startled from its slumbers by the loud summons of a telegraphic messenger. The air had been heavy all day with rumors of battle, and thousands and tens of thousands had walked the streets with throbbing hearts, in dread anticipation of the tidings any hour might bring.

We rose hastily, and presently the messenger was admitted. I took the envelope from his hand, opened it, and read:

HAGERSTOWN 17th

To___________ H ______

Capt H______ wounded shot through the neck thought not mortal at Keedysville WILLIAM G. LEDUC

Through the neck,—no bullet left in wound. Windpipe, food-pipe, carotid, jugular, half a dozen smaller, but still formidable vessels, a great braid of nerves, each as big as a lamp-wick, spinal cord,—ought to kill at once, if at all. Thought not mortal, or not thought mortal,—which was it? The first; that is better than the second would be.—"Keedysville, a post-office, Washington Co., Maryland." Leduc? Leduc? Don't remember that name. The boy is waiting for his money. A dollar and thirteen cents. Has nobody got thirteen cents? Don't keep that boy waiting,—how do we know what messages he has got to carry?

The boy had another message to carry. It was to the father of Lieutenant-Colonel Wilder Dwight, informing him that his son was grievously wounded in the same battle, and was lying at Boonsborough, a town a few miles this side of Keedysville. This I learned the next morning from the civil and attentive officials at the Central Telegraph Office.

Calling upon this gentleman, I found that he meant to leave in the quarter past two o'clock train, taking with him Dr. George H. Gay, an accomplished and energetic surgeon, equal to any difficult question or pressing emergency. I agreed to accompany them, and we met in the cars. I felt myself peculiarly fortunate in having companions whose society would be a pleasure, whose feelings would harmonize with my own, and whose assistance I might, in case of need, be glad to claim.

It is of the journey which we began together, and which I finished apart, that I mean to give my "Atlantic" readers an account. They must let me tell my story in my own way, speaking of many little matters that interested or amused me, and which a certain leisurely class of elderly persons, who sit at their firesides and never travel, will, I hope, follow with a kind of interest. For, besides the main object of my excursion, I could not help being excited by the incidental sights and occurrences of a trip which to a commercial traveller or a newspaper-reporter would seem quite commonplace and undeserving of record. There are periods in which all places and people seem to be in a conspiracy to impress us with their individuality, in which every ordinary locality seems to assume a special significance and to claim a particular notice, in which every person we meet is either an old acquaintance or a character; days in which the strangest coincidences are continually happening, so that they get to be the rule, and not the exception. Some might naturally think that anxiety and the weariness of a prolonged search after a near relative would have prevented my taking any interest in or paying any regard to the little matters around me. Perhaps it had just the contrary effect, and acted like a diffused stimulus upon the attention. When all the faculties are wide-awake in pursuit of a single object, or fixed in the spasm of an absorbing emotion, they are oftentimes clairvoyant in a marvellous degree in respect to many collateral things, as Wordsworth has so forcibly illustrated in his sonnet on the Boy of Windermere, and as Hawthorne has developed with such metaphysical accuracy in that chapter of his wondrous story where Hester walks forth to meet her punishment.

Be that as it may,—though I set out with a full and heavy heart, though many times my blood chilled with what were perhaps needless and unwise fears, though I broke through all my habits without thinking about them, which is almost as hard in certain circumstances as for one of our young fellows to leave his sweetheart and go into a Peninsular campaign, though I did not always know when I was hungry nor discover that I was thirsting, though I had a worrying ache and inward tremor underlying all the outward play of the senses and the mind, yet it is the simple truth that I did look out of the car-windows with an eye for all that passed, that I did take cognizance of strange sights and singular people, that I did act much as persons act from the ordinary promptings of curiosity, and from time to time even laugh very much as others do who are attacked with a convulsive sense of the ridiculous, the epilepsy of the diaphragm.

By a mutual compact, we talked little in the cars. A communicative friend is the greatest nuisance to have at one's side during a railroad journey, especially if his conversation is stimulating and in itself agreeable. "A fast train and a 'slow' neighbor," is my motto. Many times, when I have got upon the cars, expecting to be magnetized into an hour or two of blissful reverie, my thoughts shaken up by the vibrations into all sorts of new and pleasing patterns, arranging themselves in curves and nodal points, like the grains of sand in Chladni's famous experiment,—fresh ideas coming up to the surface, as the kernels do when a measure of corn is jolted in a farmer's wagon,—all this without volition, the mechanical impulse alone keeping the thoughts in motion, as the mere act of carrying certain watches in the pocket keeps them wound up,—many times, I say, just as my brain was beginning to creep and hum with this delicious locomotive intoxication, some dear detestable friend, cordial, intelligent, social, radiant, has come up and sat down by me and opened a conversation which has broken my day-dream, unharnessed the flying horses that were whirling along my fancies and hitched on the old weary omnibus-team of every-day associations, fatigued my hearing and attention, exhausted my voice, and milked the breasts of my thought dry during the hour when they should have been filling themselves full of fresh juices. My friends spared me this trial.

So, then, I sat by the window and enjoyed the slight tipsiness produced by short, limited, rapid oscillations, which I take to be the exhilarating stage of that condition which reaches hopeless inebriety in what we know as sea-sickness. Where the horizon opened widely, it pleased me to watch the curious effect of the rapid movement of near objects contrasted with the slow motion of distant ones. Looking from a right-hand window, for instance, the fences close by glide swiftly backward, or to the right, while the distant hills not only do not appear to move backward, but look by contrast with the fences near at hand as if they were moving forward, or to the left; and thus the whole landscape becomes a mighty wheel revolving about an imaginary axis somewhere in the middle-distance.

My companions proposed to stay at one of the best-known and longest-established of the New-York caravansaries, and I accompanied them. We were particularly well lodged, and not uncivilly treated. The traveller who supposes that he is to repeat the melancholy experience of Shenstone, and have to sigh over the reflection that he has found "his warmest welcome at an inn," has something to learn at the offices of the great city hotels. The unheralded guest who is honored by mere indifference may think himself blessed with singular good-fortune. If the despot of the Patent-Annunciator is only mildly contemptuous in his manner, let the victim look upon it as a personal favor. The coldest welcome that a threadbare curate ever got at the door of a bishop's palace, the most icy reception that a country cousin ever received at the city mansion of a mushroom millionaire, is agreeably tepid, compared to that which the Rhadamanthus who dooms you to the more or less elevated circle of his inverted Inferno vouchsafes, as you step up to enter your name on his dog's-eared register. I have less hesitation in unburdening myself of this uncomfortable statement, as on this particular trip I met with more than one exception to the rule. Officials become brutalized, I suppose, as a matter of course. One cannot expect an office clerk to embrace tenderly every stranger who comes in with a carpet-bag, or a telegraph operator to burst into tears over every unpleasant message he receives for transmission. Still, humanity is not always totally extinguished in these persons. I discovered a youth in a telegraph office of the Continental Hotel, in Philadelphia, who was as pleasant in conversation, and as graciously responsive to inoffensive questions, as if I had been his childless opulent uncle and my will not made.

On the road again the next morning, over the ferry, into the cars with sliding panels and fixed windows, so that in summer the whole side of the car may be made transparent. New Jersey is, to the apprehension of a traveller, a double-headed suburb rather than a State. Its dull red dust looks like the dried and powdered mud of a battle-field. Peach-trees are common, and champagne-orchards. Canal-boats, drawn by mules, swim by, feeling their way along like blind men led by dogs. I had a mighty passion come over me to be the captain of one,—to glide back and forward upon a sea never roughened by storms,—to float where I could not sink,—to navigate where there is no shipwreck,—to lie languidly on the deck and govern the huge craft by a word or the movement of a finger: there was something of railroad intoxication in the fancy: but who has not often envied a cobbler in his stall?

The boys cry the "N'-York Heddle," instead of "Herald"; I remember that years ago in Philadelphia; we must be getting near the farther end of the dumb-bell suburb. A bridge has been swept away by a rise of the waters, so we must approach Philadelphia by the river. Her physiognomy is not distinguished; nez camus, as a Frenchman would say; no illustrious steeple, no imposing tower; the water-edge of the town looking bedraggled, like the flounce of a vulgar rich woman's dress that trails on the sidewalk. The New Ironsides lies at one of the wharves, elephantine in bulk and color, her sides narrowing as they rise, like the walls of a hock-glass.

I went straight to the house in Walnut Street where the Captain would be heard of, if anywhere in this region. His lieutenant-colonel was there, gravely wounded; his college-friend and comrade in arms, a son of the house, was there, injured in a similar way; another soldier, brother of the last, was there, prostrate with fever. A fourth bed was waiting ready for the Captain, but not one word had been heard of him, though inquiries had been made in the towns from and through which the father had brought his two sons and the lieutenant-colonel. And so my search is, like a "Ledger" story, to be continued.

I rejoined my companions in time to take the noon-train for Baltimore. Our company was gaining in number as it moved onwards. We had found upon the train from New York a lovely, lonely lady, the wife of one of our most spirited Massachusetts officers, the brave Colonel of the __th Regiment, going to seek her wounded husband at Middletown, a place lying directly in our track. She was the light of our party while we were together on our pilgrimage, a fair, gracious woman, gentle, but courageous,

> — *"ful plesant and amiable of port,*
>
> —*estatelich of manere,*
>
> *And to ben holden digne of reverence."*

On the road from Philadelphia, I found in the same car with our party Dr. William Hunt of Philadelphia, who had most kindly and faithfully attended the Captain, then the Lieutenant, after a wound received at Ball's Bluff, which came very near being mortal. He was going upon an errand of mercy to the wounded, and found he had in his memorandum-book the name of our lady's husband, the Colonel, who had been commended to his particular attention.

Not long after leaving Philadelphia, we passed a solitary sentry keeping guard over a short railroad bridge. It was the first evidence that we were approaching the perilous borders, the marches where the North and the South mingle their angry hosts, where the extremes of our so-called civilization meet in conflict, and the fierce slave-driver of the Lower Mississippi stares into the stern eyes of the forest-feller from the banks of the Aroostook. All the way along, the bridges were guarded more or less strongly. In a vast country like ours, communications play a far more complex part than in Europe, where the whole territory available for strategic purposes is so comparatively limited. Belgium, for instance, has long been the bowling-alley where kings roll cannon-balls at each other's armies; but here we are playing the game of live ninepins without any alley.

We were obliged to stay in Baltimore over night, as we were too late for the train to Frederick. At the Eutaw House, where we found both comfort and courtesy, we met a number of friends, who beguiled the evening hours for us in the most agreeable manner. We devoted some time to procuring surgical and other articles, such as might be useful to our friends, or to others, if our friends should not need them. In the morning, I found myself seated at the breakfast-table next to General Wool. It did not surprise me to find the General very far from expansive. With Fort McHenry on his shoulders and

Baltimore in his breeches-pocket, and the weight of a military department loading down his social safety-valves, I thought it a great deal for an officer in his trying position to select so very obliging and affable an aid as the gentleman who relieved him of the burden of attending to strangers.

We left the Eutaw House, to take the cars for Frederick. As we stood waiting on the platform, a telegraphic message was handed in silence to my companion. Sad news: the lifeless body of the son he was hastening to see was even now on its way to him in Baltimore. It was no time for empty words of consolation: I knew what he had lost, and that now was not the time to intrude upon a grief borne as men bear it, felt as women feel it.

Colonel Wilder Dwight was first made known to me as the friend of a beloved relative of my own, who was with him during a severe illness in Switzerland; and for whom while living, and for whose memory when dead, he retained the warmest affection. Since that the story of his noble deeds of daring, of his capture and escape, and a brief visit home before he was able to rejoin his regiment, had made his name familiar to many among us, myself among the number. His memory has been honored by those who had the largest opportunity of knowing his rare promise, as a man of talents and energy of nature. His abounding vitality must have produced its impression on all who met him; there was a still fire about him which any one could see would blaze up to melt all difficulties and recast obstacles into implements in the mould of an heroic will. These elements of his character many had the chance of knowing; but I shall always associate him with the memory of that pure and noble friendship which made me feel that I knew him before I looked upon his face, and added a personal tenderness to the sense of loss which I share with the whole community.

Here, then, I parted, sorrowfully, from the companions with whom I set out on my journey.

In one of the cars, at the same station, we met General Shriver of Frederick, a most loyal Unionist, whose name is synonymous with a hearty welcome to all whom he can aid by his counsel and his hospitality. He took great pains to give us all the information we needed, and expressed the hope, which was afterwards fulfilled, to the great gratification of some of us, that we should meet again when he should return to his home.

There was nothing worthy of special note in the trip to Frederick, except our passing a squad of Rebel prisoners, whom I missed seeing, as they flashed by, but who were said to be a most forlorn-looking crowd of scarecrows. Arrived at the Monocacy River, about three miles this side of Frederick, we came to a halt, for the railroad bridge had been blown up by the Rebels, and its iron pillars and arches were lying in the bed of the river.

The unfortunate wretch who fired the train was killed by the explosion, and lay buried hard by, his hands sticking out of the shallow grave into which he had been huddled. This was the story they told us, but whether true or not I must leave to the correspondents of "Notes and Queries" to settle.

There was a great confusion of carriages and wagons at the stopping-place of the train, so that it was a long time before I could get anything that would carry us. At last I was lucky enough to light on a sturdy wagon, drawn by a pair of serviceable bays, and driven by James Grayden, with whom I was destined to have a somewhat continued acquaintance. We took up a little girl who had been in Baltimore during the late Rebel inroad. It made me think of the time when my own mother, at that time six years old, was hurried off from Boston, then occupied by the British soldiers, to Newburyport, and heard the people saying that "the redcoats were coming, killing and murdering everybody as they went along." Frederick looked cheerful for a place that had so recently been in an enemy's hands. Here and there a house or shop was shut up, but the national colors were waving in all directions, and the general aspect was peaceful and contented. I saw no bullet-marks or other sign of the fighting which had gone on in the streets. The Colonel's lady was taken in charge by a daughter of that hospitable family to which we had been commended by its head, and I proceeded to inquire for wounded officers at the various temporary hospitals.

At the United States Hotel, where many were lying, I heard mention of an officer in an upper chamber, and, going there, found Lieutenant Abbott, of the Twentieth Massachusetts Volunteers, lying ill with what looked like typhoid fever. While there, who should come in but the almost ubiquitous Lieutenant Wilkins, of the same Twentieth, whom I had met repeatedly before on errands of kindness or duty, and who was just from the battle-ground. He was going to Boston in charge of the body of the lamented Dr. Revere, the Assistant Surgeon of the regiment, killed on the field. From his lips I learned something of the mishaps of the regiment. My Captain's wound he spoke of as less grave than at first thought; but he mentioned incidentally having heard a story recently that he was killed,—a fiction, doubtless,—a mistake,—a palpable absurdity,—not to be remembered or made any account of. Oh no! but what dull ache is this in that obscurely sensitive region, somewhere below the heart, where the nervous centre called the semilunar ganglion lies unconscious of itself until a great grief or a mastering anxiety reaches it through all the non-conductors which isolate it from ordinary impressions? I talked awhile with Lieutenant Abbott, who lay prostrate, feeble, but soldier-like and uncomplaining, carefully waited upon by a most excellent lady, a captain's wife, New England born, loyal as the Liberty on a golden ten-dollar piece, and of lofty bearing enough to have sat for that goddess's portrait. She had stayed in Frederick through the Rebel inroad, and kept the star-spangled banner where it would be safe, to unroll it as the last Rebel hoofs clattered off from the pavement of the town.

Near by Lieutenant Abbott was an unhappy gentleman, occupying a small chamber, and filling it with his troubles. When he gets well and plump, I know he will forgive me if I confess that I could not help smiling in the midst of my sympathy for him. He had been a well-favored man, he said, sweeping his hand in a semicircle, which implied that his acute-angled countenance had once filled the goodly curve he described. He was now a perfect Don Quixote to look upon. Weakness had made him querulous, as it does all of us, and he piped his grievances to me in a thin voice, with that finish of detail which chronic invalidism alone can command. He was starving,—he could not get what he wanted to eat. He was in need of stimulants, and he held up a pitiful two-ounce phial containing three thimblefuls—of brandy,—his whole stock of that encouraging article. Him I consoled to the best of my ability, and afterwards, in some slight measure, supplied his wants. Feed this poor gentleman up, as these good people soon will, and I should not know him, nor he himself. We are all egotists in sickness and debility. An animal has been defined as "a stomach ministered to by organs;" and the greatest man comes very near this simple formula after a month or two of fever and starvation.

James Grayden and his team pleased me well enough, and so I made a bargain with him to take us, the lady and myself, on our further journey as far as Middletown. As we were about starting from the front of the United States Hotel, two gentlemen presented themselves and expressed a wish to be allowed to share our conveyance. I looked at them and convinced myself that they were neither Rebels in disguise, nor deserters, nor camp-followers, nor miscreants, but plain, honest men on a proper errand. The first of them I will pass over briefly. He was a young man of mild and modest demeanor, chaplain to a Pennsylvania regiment, which he was going to rejoin. He belonged to the Moravian Church, of which I had the misfortune to know little more than what I had learned from Southey's "Life of Wesley." and from the exquisite hymns we have borrowed from its rhapsodists. The other stranger was a New Englander of respectable appearance, with a grave, hard, honest, hay-bearded face, who had come to serve the sick and wounded on the battle-field and in its immediate neighborhood. There is no reason why I should not mention his name, but I shall content myself with calling him the Philanthropist.

So we set forth, the sturdy wagon, the serviceable bays, with James Grayden their driver, the gentle lady, whose serene patience bore up through all delays and discomforts, the Chaplain, the Philanthropist, and myself, the teller of this story.

And now, as we emerged from Frederick, we struck at once upon the trail from the great battle-field. The road was filled with straggling and wounded soldiers. All who could travel on foot,—multitudes with slight wounds of the upper limbs, the head, or face,—were told to take up their beds,—a light burden or none at all,—and walk. Just as the battle-field sucks everything into its red vortex for the conflict, so does it drive everything off in long, diverging rays after the fierce centripetal forces have met and neutralized each other. For more than a week there had been sharp fighting all along this road. Through the streets of Frederick, through Crampton's Gap, over South Mountain, sweeping at last the hills and the woods that skirt the windings of the Antietam, the long battle had travelled, like one of those tornadoes which tear their path through our fields and villages. The slain of higher condition, "embalmed" and iron-cased, were sliding off on the railways to their far homes; the dead of the rank and file were being gathered up and committed hastily to the earth; the gravely wounded were cared for hard by the scene of conflict, or pushed a little way along to the neighboring villages; while those who could walk were meeting us, as I have said, at every step in the road. It was a pitiable sight, truly pitiable, yet so vast, so far beyond the possibility of relief, that many single sorrows of small dimensions have wrought upon my feelings more than the sight of this great caravan of maimed pilgrims. The companionship of so many seemed to make a joint-stock of their suffering; it was next to impossible to individualize it, and so bring it home, as one can do with a single broken limb or aching wound. Then they were all of the male sex, and in the freshness or the prime of their strength. Though they tramped so wearily along, yet there was rest and kind nursing in store for them. These wounds they bore would be the medals they would show their children and grandchildren by and by. Who would not rather wear his decorations beneath his uniform than on it?

Yet among them were figures which arrested our attention and sympathy. Delicate boys, with more spirit than strength, flushed with fever or pale with exhaustion or haggard with suffering, dragged their weary limbs along as if each step would exhaust their slender store of strength. At the roadside sat or lay others, quite spent with their journey. Here and there was a house at which the wayfarers would stop, in the hope, I fear often vain, of getting refreshment; and in one place was a clear, cool spring, where the little bands of the long procession halted for a few moments, as the trains that traverse the desert rest by its fountains. My companions had brought a few peaches along with them, which the Philanthropist bestowed upon the tired and thirsty soldiers with a satisfaction which we all shared. I had with me a small flask of strong waters, to be used as a medicine in case of inward grief. From this, also, he dispensed relief, without hesitation, to a poor fellow who looked as if he needed it. I rather admired the simplicity with which he applied my limited means of solace to the first-comer who wanted it more than I; a genuine benevolent impulse does not stand on ceremony, and had I perished of colic for want of a stimulus that night, I should not have reproached my friend the Philanthropist, any more than I grudged my other ardent friend the two dollars and more which it cost me to send the charitable message he left in my hands.

It was a lovely country through which we were riding. The hillsides rolled away into the distance, slanting up fair and broad to the sun, as one sees them in the open parts of the Berkshire Valley, at Lanesborough, for instance, or in the many-hued mountain chalice at the bottom of which the Shaker houses of Lebanon have shaped themselves like a sediment of cubical crystals. The wheat was all garnered, and the land ploughed for a new crop. There was Indian corn standing, but I saw no pumpkins warming their yellow carapaces in the sunshine like so many turtles; only in a single instance did I notice some wretched little miniature specimens in form and hue not unlike those colossal oranges of our cornfields. The rail fences were somewhat disturbed, and the cinders of extinguished fires showed the use to which they had been applied. The houses along the road were not for the most part neatly kept; the garden fences were poorly built of laths or long slats, and very rarely of trim aspect. The men of this region seemed to ride in the saddle very generally, rather than drive. They looked sober and stern, less curious and lively than Yankees, and I fancied that a type of features familiar to us in the countenance of the late John Tyler, our accidental President, was frequently met with. The women were still more distinguishable from our New England pattern. Soft, sallow, succulent, delicately finished about the mouth and firmly shaped about the chin, dark-eyed, full-throated, they looked as if they had been grown in a land of olives. There was a little toss in their movement, full of muliebrity. I fancied there was something more of the duck and less of the chicken about them, as compared with the daughters of our leaner soil; but these are mere impressions caught from stray glances, and if there is any offence in them, my fair readers may consider them all retracted.

At intervals, a dead horse lay by the roadside, or in the fields, unburied, not grateful to gods or men. I saw no bird of prey, no ill-omened fowl, on my way to the carnival of death, or at the place where it had been held. The vulture of story, the crow of Talavera, the "twa corbies" of the ghastly ballad, are all from Nature, doubtless; but no black wing was spread over these animal ruins, and no call to the banquet pierced through the heavy-laden and sickening air.

Full in the middle of the road, caring little for whom or what they met, came long strings of army wagons, returning empty from the front after supplies. James Grayden stated it as his conviction that they had a little rather run into a fellow than not. I liked the looks of these equipages and their drivers; they meant business. Drawn by mules mostly, six, I think, to a wagon, powdered well with dust, wagon, beast, and driver, they came jogging along the road, turning neither to right nor left,—some driven by bearded, solemn white men, some by careless, saucy-looking negroes, of a blackness like that of anthracite or obsidian. There seemed to be nothing about them, dead or alive, that was not serviceable. Sometimes a mule would give out on the road; then he was left where he lay, until by and by he would think better of it, and get up, when the first public wagon that came along would hitch him on, and restore him to the sphere of duty.

It was evening when we got to Middletown. The gentle lady who had graced our homely conveyance with her company here left us. She found her husband, the gallant Colonel, in very comfortable quarters, well cared for, very weak from the effects of the fearful operation he had been compelled to undergo, but showing calm courage to endure as he had shown manly energy to act. It was a meeting full of heroism and tenderness, of which I heard more than there is need to tell. Health to the brave soldier, and peace to the household over which so fair a spirit presides!

Dr. Thompson, the very active and intelligent surgical director of the hospitals of the place, took me in charge. He carried me to the house of a worthy and benevolent clergyman of the German Reformed Church, where I was to take tea and pass the night. What became of the Moravian chaplain I did not know; but my friend the Philanthropist had evidently made up his mind to adhere to my fortunes. He followed me, therefore, to the house of the "Dominie," as a newspaper correspondent calls my kind host, and partook of the fare there furnished me. He withdrew with me to the apartment assigned for my slumbers, and slept sweetly on the same pillow where I waked and tossed. Nay, I do affirm that he did, unconsciously, I believe, encroach on that moiety of the couch which I had flattered myself was to be my own through the watches of the night, and that I was in serious doubt at one time whether I should not be gradually, but irresistibly, expelled from the bed which I had supposed destined for my sole possession. As Ruth clave unto Naomi, so my friend the Philanthropist clave unto me. "Whither thou goest, I will go; and where thou lodgest, I will lodge." A really kind, good man, full of zeal, determined to help somebody, and absorbed in his one thought, he doubted nobody's willingness to serve him, going, as he was, on a purely benevolent errand. When he reads this, as I hope he will, let him be assured of my esteem and respect; and if he gained any accommodation from being in my company, let me tell him that I learned a lesson from his active benevolence. I could, however, have wished to hear him laugh once before we parted, perhaps forever. He did not, to the best of my recollection, even smile during the whole period that we were in company. I am afraid that a lightsome disposition and a relish for humor are not so common in those whose benevolence takes an active turn as in people of sentiment, who are always ready with their tears and abounding in passionate expressions of sympathy. Working philanthropy is a practical specialty, requiring not a mere impulse, but a talent, with its peculiar sagacity for finding its objects, a tact for selecting its agencies, an organizing and arranging faculty, a steady set of nerves, and a constitution such as Sallust describes in Catiline, patient of cold, of hunger, and of watching. Philanthropists are commonly grave, occasionally grim, and not very rarely morose. Their expansive social force is imprisoned as a working power, to show itself only through its legitimate pistons and cranks. The tighter the boiler, the less it whistles and sings at its work. When Dr. Waterhouse, in 1780, travelled with Howard, on his tour among the Dutch prisons and hospitals, he found his temper and manners very different from what would have been expected.

My benevolent companion having already made a preliminary exploration of the hospitals of the place, before sharing my bed with him, as above mentioned, I joined him in a second tour through them. The authorities of Middletown are evidently leagued with the surgeons of that place, for such a break-neck succession of pitfalls and chasms I have never seen in the streets of a civilized town. It was getting late in the evening when we began our rounds. The principal collections of the wounded were in the churches. Boards were laid over the tops of the pews, on these some straw was spread, and on this the wounded lay, with little or no covering other than such scanty clothes as they had on. There were wounds of all degrees of severity, but I heard no groans or murmurs. Most of the sufferers were hurt in the limbs, some had undergone amputation, and all had, I presume, received such attention as was required. Still, it was but a rough and dreary kind of comfort that the extemporized hospitals suggested. I could not help thinking the patients must be cold; but they were used to camp life, and did not complain. The men who watched were not of the soft-handed variety of the race. One of them was smoking his pipe as he went from bed to bed. I saw one poor fellow who had been shot through the breast; his breathing was labored, and he was tossing, anxious and restless. The men were debating about the opiate he was to take, and I was thankful that I happened there at the right moment to see that he was well narcotized for the night. Was it possible that my Captain could be lying on the straw in one of these places? Certainly possible, but not probable; but as the lantern was held over each bed, it was with a kind of thrill that I looked upon the features it illuminated. Many times as I went from hospital to hospital in my wanderings, I started as some faint resemblance,--the shade of a young man's hair, the outline of his half-turned face,—recalled the presence I was in search of. The face would turn towards me, and the momentary illusion would pass away, but still the fancy clung to me. There was no figure huddled up on its rude couch, none stretched at the roadside, none toiling languidly along the dusty pike, none passing in car or in ambulance, that I did not scrutinize, as if it might be that for which I was making my pilgrimage to the battlefield.

"There are two wounded Secesh," said my companion. I walked to the bedside of the first, who was an officer, a lieutenant, if I remember right, from North Carolina. He was of good family, son of a judge in one of the higher courts of his State, educated, pleasant, gentle, intelligent. One moment's intercourse with such an enemy, lying helpless and wounded among strangers, takes away all personal bitterness towards those with whom we or our children have been but a few hours before in deadly strife. The basest lie which the murderous contrivers of this Rebellion have told is that which tries to make out a difference of race in the men of the North and South. It would be worth a year of battles to abolish this delusion, though the great sponge of war that wiped it out were moistened with the best blood of the land. My Rebel was of slight, scholastic habit, and spoke as one accustomed to tread carefully among the parts of speech. It made my heart ache to see him, a man finished in the humanities and Christian culture, whom the sin of his forefathers and the crime of his rulers had set in barbarous conflict against others of like training with his own,—a man who, but for the curse which our generation is called on to expiate, would have taken his part in the beneficent task of shaping the intelligence and lifting the moral standard of a peaceful and united people.

On Sunday morning, the twenty-first, having engaged James Grayden and his team, I set out with the Chaplain and the Philanthropist for Keedysville. Our track lay through the South Mountain Gap, and led us first to the town of Boonsborough, where, it will be remembered, Colonel Dwight had been brought after the battle. We saw the positions occupied in the battle of South Mountain, and many traces of the conflict. In one situation a group of young trees was marked with shot, hardly one having escaped. As we walked by the side of the wagon, the Philanthropist left us for a while and climbed a hill, where, along the line of a fence, he found traces of the most desperate fighting. A ride of some three hours brought us to Boonsborough, where I roused the unfortunate army surgeon who had charge of the hospitals, and who was trying to get a little sleep after his fatigues and watchings. He bore this cross very creditably, and helped me to explore all places where my soldier might be lying among the crowds of wounded. After the useless search, I resumed my journey, fortified with a note of introduction to Dr. Letterman; also with a bale of oakum which I was to carry to that gentleman, this substance being employed as a substitute for lint. We were obliged also to procure a pass to Keedysville from the Provost Marshal of Boonsborough. As we came near the place, we learned that General McClellan's head quarters had been removed from this village some miles farther to the front.

On entering the small settlement of Keedysville, a familiar face and figure blocked the way, like one of Bunyan's giants. The tall form and benevolent countenance, set off by long, flowing hair, belonged to the excellent Mayor Frank B. Fay of Chelsea, who, like my Philanthropist, only still more promptly, had come to succor the wounded of the great battle. It was wonderful to see how his single personality pervaded this torpid little village; he seemed to be the centre of all its activities. All my questions he answered clearly and decisively, as one who knew everything that was going on in the place. But the one question I had come five hundred miles to ask,—Where is Captain H.?—he could not answer. There were some thousands of wounded in the place, he told me, scattered about everywhere. It would be a long job to hunt up my Captain; the only way would be to go to every house and ask for him. Just then a medical officer came up.

"Do you know anything of Captain H. of the Massachusetts Twentieth?"

"Oh yes; he is staying in that house. I saw him there, doing very well."

A chorus of hallelujahs arose in my soul, but I kept them to myself. Now, then, for our twice-wounded volunteer, our young centurion whose double-barred shoulder-straps we have never yet looked upon. Let us observe the proprieties, however; no swelling upward of the mother,—no hysterica passio, we do not like scenes. A calm salutation,—then swallow and hold hard. That is about the programme.

A cottage of squared logs, filled in with plaster, and whitewashed. A little yard before it, with a gate swinging. The door of the cottage ajar,—no one visible as yet. I push open the door and enter. An old woman, Margaret Kitzmuller her name proves to be, is the first person I see.

"Captain H. here?"

"Oh no, sir,—left yesterday morning for Hagerstown,—in a milk-cart."

The Kitzmuller is a beady-eyed, cheery-looking ancient woman, answers questions with a rising inflection, and gives a good account of the Captain, who got into the vehicle without assistance, and was in excellent spirits. Of course he had struck for Hagerstown as the terminus of the Cumberland Valley Railroad, and was on his way to Philadelphia, via Chambersburg and Harrisburg, if he were not already in the hospitable home of Walnut Street, where his friends were expecting him.

I might follow on his track or return upon my own; the distance was the same to Philadelphia through Harrisburg as through Baltimore. But it was very difficult, Mr. Fay told me, to procure any kind of conveyance to Hagerstown; and, on the other hand, I had James Grayden and his wagon to carry me back to Frederick. It was not likely that I should overtake the object of my pursuit with nearly thirty-six hours start, even if I could procure a conveyance that day. In the mean time James was getting impatient to be on his return, according to the direction of his employers. So I decided to go back with him.

But there was the great battle-field only about three miles from Keedysville, and it was impossible to go without seeing that. James Grayden's directions were peremptory, but it was a case for the higher law. I must make a good offer for an extra couple of hours, such as would satisfy the owners of the wagon, and enforce it by a personal motive. I did this handsomely, and succeeded without difficulty. To add brilliancy to my enterprise, I invited the Chaplain and the Philanthropist to take a free passage with me.

We followed the road through the village for a space, then turned off to the right, and wandered somewhat vaguely, for want of precise directions, over the hills. Inquiring as we went, we forded a wide creek in which soldiers were washing their clothes, the name of which we did not then know, but which must have been the Antietam. At one point we met a party, women among them, bringing off various trophies they had picked up on the battlefield. Still wandering along, we were at last pointed to a hill in the distance, a part of the summit of which was covered with Indian corn. There, we were told, some of the fiercest fighting of the day had been done. The fences were taken down so as to make a passage across the fields, and the tracks worn within the last few days looked like old roads. We passed a fresh grave under a tree near the road. A board was nailed to the tree, bearing the name, as well as I could make it out, of Gardiner, of a New Hampshire regiment.

On coming near the brow of the hill, we met a party carrying picks and spades. "How many?" "Only one." The dead were nearly all buried, then, in this region of the field of strife. We stopped the wagon, and, getting out, began to look around us. Hard by was a large pile of muskets, scores, if not hundreds, which had been picked up, and were guarded for the Government. A long ridge of fresh gravel rose before us. A board stuck up in front of it bore this inscription, the first part of which was, I believe, not correct: "The Rebel General Anderson and 80 Rebels are buried in this hole." Other smaller ridges were marked with the number of dead lying under them. The whole ground was strewed with fragments of clothing, haversacks, canteens, cap-boxes, bullets, cartridge-boxes, cartridges, scraps of paper, portions of bread and meat. I saw two soldiers' caps that looked as though their owners had been shot through the head. In several places I noticed dark red patches where a pool of blood had curdled and caked, as some poor fellow poured his life out on the sod. I then wandered about in the cornfield. It surprised me to notice, that, though there was every mark of hard fighting having taken place here, the Indian corn was not generally trodden down. One of our cornfields is a kind of forest, and even when fighting, men avoid the tall stalks as if they were trees. At the edge of this cornfield lay a gray horse, said to have belonged to a Rebel colonel, who was killed near the same place. Not far off were two dead artillery horses in their harness. Another had been attended to by a burying-party, who had thrown some earth over him but his last bed-clothes were too short, and his legs stuck out stark and stiff from beneath the gravel coverlet. It was a great pity that we had no intelligent guide to explain to us the position of that portion of the two armies which fought over this ground. There was a shallow trench before we came to the cornfield, too narrow for a road, as I should think, too elevated for a water-course, and which seemed to have been used as a rifle-pit. At any rate, there had been hard fighting in and about it. This and the cornfield may serve to identify the part of the ground we visited, if any who fought there should ever look over this paper. The opposing tides of battle must have blended their waves at this point, for portions of gray uniform were mingled with the "garments rolled in blood" torn from our own dead and wounded soldiers. I picked up a Rebel canteen, and one of our own,—but there was something repulsive about the trodden and stained relics of the stale battle-field. It was like the table of some hideous orgy left uncleared, and one turned away disgusted from its broken fragments and muddy heeltaps. A bullet or two, a button, a brass plate from a soldier's belt, served well enough for mementos of my visit, with a letter which I picked up, directed to Richmond, Virginia, its seal unbroken. "N. C. Cleveland County. F. Wright to J. Wright." On the other side, "A few lines from W. L. Vaughn." who has just been writing for the wife to her husband, and continues on his own account. The postscript, "tell John that nancy's folks are all well and has a verry good Little Crop of corn a growing." I wonder, if, by one of those strange chances of which I have seen so many, this number or leaf of the "Atlantic" will not sooner or later find its way to Cleveland County, North Carolina, and E. Wright, widow of James Wright, and Nancy's folks, get from these sentences the last glimpse of husband and friend as he threw up his arms and fell in the bloody cornfield of Antietam? I will keep this stained letter for them until peace comes back, if it comes in my time, and my pleasant North Carolina Rebel of the Middletown Hospital will, perhaps look these poor people up, and tell them where to send for it.

On the battle-field I parted with my two companions, the Chaplain and the Philanthropist. They were going to the front, the one to find his regiment, the other to look for those who needed his assistance. We exchanged cards and farewells, I mounted the wagon, the horses' heads were turned homewards, my two companions went their way, and I saw them no more. On my way back, I fell into talk with James Grayden. Born in England, Lancashire; in this country since he was four years old. Had nothing to care for but an old mother; didn't know what he should do if he lost her. Though so long in this country, he had all the simplicity and childlike lightheartedness which belong to the Old World's people. He laughed at the smallest pleasantry, and showed his great white English teeth; he took a joke without retorting by an impertinence; he had a very limited curiosity about all that was going on; he had small store of information; he lived chiefly in his horses, it seemed to me. His quiet animal nature acted as a pleasing anodyne to my recurring fits of anxiety, and I liked his frequent "'Deed I don't know, sir." better than I have sometimes relished the large discourse of professors and other very wise men.

I have not much to say of the road which we were travelling for the second time. Reaching Middletown, my first call was on the wounded Colonel and his lady. She gave me a most touching account of all the suffering he had gone through with his shattered limb before he succeeded in finding a shelter; showing the terrible want of proper means of transportation of the wounded after the battle. It occurred to me, while at this house, that I was more or less famished, and for the first time in my life I begged for a meal, which the kind family with whom the Colonel was staying most graciously furnished me.

After tea, there came in a stout army surgeon, a Highlander by birth, educated in Edinburgh, with whom I had pleasant, not unstimulating talk. He had been brought very close to that immane and nefandous Burke-and-Hare business which made the blood of civilization run cold in the year 1828, and told me, in a very calm way, with an occasional pinch from the mull, to refresh his memory, some of the details of those frightful murders, never rivalled in horror until the wretch Dumollard, who kept a private cemetery for his victims, was dragged into the light of day. He had a good deal to say, too, about the Royal College of Surgeons in Edinburgh, and the famous preparations, mercurial and the rest, which I remember well having seen there,—the "sudabit multum," and others,—also of our New York Professor Carnochan's handiwork, a specimen of which I once admired at the New York College. But the doctor was not in a happy frame of mind, and seemed willing to forget the present in the past: things went wrong, somehow, and the time was out of joint with him.

Dr. Thompson, kind, cheerful, companionable, offered me half his own wide bed, in the house of Dr. Baer, for my second night in Middletown. Here I lay awake again another night. Close to the house stood an ambulance in which was a wounded Rebel officer, attended by one of their own surgeons. He was calling out in a loud voice, all night long, as it seemed to me, "Doctor! Doctor! Driver! Water!" in loud, complaining tones, I have no doubt of real suffering, but in strange contrast with the silent patience which was the almost universal rule.

The courteous Dr. Thompson will let me tell here an odd coincidence, trivial, but having its interest as one of a series. The Doctor and myself lay in the bed, and a lieutenant, a friend of his, slept on the sofa, At night, I placed my match-box, a Scotch one, of the Macpherson-plaid pattern, which I bought years ago, on the bureau, just where I could put my hand upon it. I was the last of the three to rise in the morning, and on looking for my pretty match-box, I found it was gone. This was rather awkward,—not on account of the loss, but of the unavoidable fact that one of my fellow-lodgers must have taken it. I must try to find out what it meant.

"By the way, Doctor, have you seen anything of a little plaid-pattern match-box?"

The Doctor put his hand to his pocket, and, to his own huge surprise and my great gratification, pulled out two match-boxes exactly alike, both printed with the Macpherson plaid. One was his, the other mine, which he had seen lying round, and naturally took for his own, thrusting it into his pocket, where it found its twin-brother from the same workshop. In memory of which event, we exchanged boxes, like two Homeric heroes.

This curious coincidence illustrates well enough some supposed cases of plagiarism of which I will mention one where my name figured. When a little poem called "The Two Streams" was first printed, a writer in the New York "Evening Post" virtually accused the author of it of borrowing the thought from a baccalaureate sermon of President Hopkins of Williamstown, and printed a quotation from that discourse, which, as I thought, a thief or catch-poll might well consider as establishing a fair presumption that it was so borrowed. I was at the same time wholly unconscious of ever having met with the discourse or the sentence which the verses were most like, nor do I believe I ever had seen or heard either. Some time after this, happening to meet my eloquent cousin, Wendell Phillips, I mentioned the fact to him, and he told me that he had once used the special image said to be borrowed, in a discourse delivered at Williamstown. On relating this to my friend Mr. Buchanan Read, he informed me that he too, had used the image,— perhaps referring to his poem called "The Twins." He thought Tennyson had used it also. The parting of the streams on the Alps is poetically elaborated in a passage attributed to "M. Loisne," printed in the "Boston Evening Transcript" for October 23, 1859. Captain, afterwards Sir Francis Head, speaks of the showers parting on the Cordilleras, one portion going to the Atlantic, one to the Pacific. I found the image running loose in my mind, without a halter. It suggested itself as an illustration of the will, and I worked the poem out by the aid of Mitchell's School Atlas.—The spores of a great many ideas are floating about in the atmosphere. We no more know where all the growths of our mind came from, than where the lichens which eat the names off from the gravestones borrowed the germs that gave them birth. The two match-boxes were just alike, but neither was a plagiarism.

In the morning I took to the same wagon once more, but, instead of James Grayden, I was to have for my driver a young man who spelt his name "Phillip Ottenheimer" and whose features at once showed him to be an Israelite. I found him agreeable enough, and disposed to talk. So I asked him many questions about his religion, and got some answers that sound strangely in Christian ears. He was from Wittenberg, and had been educated in strict Jewish fashion. From his childhood he had read Hebrew, but was not much of a scholar otherwise. A young person of his race lost caste utterly by marrying a Christian. The Founder of our religion was considered by the Israelites to have been "a right smart man and a great doctor." But the horror with which the reading of the New Testament by any young person of their faith would be regarded was as great, I judged by his language, as that of one of our straitest sectaries would be, if he found his son or daughter perusing the "Age of Reason."

In approaching Frederick, the singular beauty of its clustered spires struck me very much, so that I was not surprised to find "Fair-View" laid down about this point on a railroad map. I wish some wandering photographer would take a picture of the place, a stereoscopic one, if possible, to show how gracefully, how charmingly, its group of steeples nestles among the Maryland hills. The town had a poetical look from a distance, as if seers and dreamers might dwell there. The first sign I read, on entering its long street, might perhaps be considered as confirming my remote impression. It bore these words: "Miss Ogle, Past, Present, and Future." On arriving, I visited Lieutenant Abbott, and the attenuated unhappy gentleman, his neighbor, sharing between them as my parting gift what I had left of the balsam known to the Pharmacopoeia as Spiritus Vini Gallici. I took advantage of General Shriver's always open door to write a letter home, but had not time to partake of his offered hospitality. The railroad bridge over the Monocacy had been rebuilt since I passed through Frederick, and we trundled along over the track toward Baltimore.

It was a disappointment, on reaching the Eutaw House, where I had ordered all communications to be addressed, to find no telegraphic message from Philadelphia or Boston, stating that Captain H. had arrived at the former place, "wound doing well in good spirits expects to leave soon for Boston." After all, it was no great matter; the Captain was, no doubt, snugly lodged before this in the house called Beautiful, at — Walnut Street, where that "grave and beautiful damsel named Discretion" had already welcomed him, smiling, though "the water stood in her eyes," and had "called out Prudence, Piety, and Charity, who, after a little more discourse with him, had him into the family."

The friends I had met at the Eutaw House had all gone but one, the lady of an officer from Boston, who was most amiable and agreeable, and whose benevolence, as I afterwards learned, soon reached the invalids I had left suffering at Frederick. General Wool still walked the corridors, inexpansive, with Fort McHenry on his shoulders, and Baltimore in his breeches-pocket, and his courteous aid again pressed upon me his kind offices. About the doors of the hotel the news-boys cried the papers in plaintive, wailing tones, as different from the sharp accents of their Boston counterparts as a sigh from the southwest is from a northeastern breeze. To understand what they said was, of course, impossible to any but an educated ear, and if I made out "Starr" and "Clipp'rr," it was because I knew beforehand what must be the burden of their advertising coranach.

I set out for Philadelphia on the morrow, Tuesday the twenty-third, there beyond question to meet my Captain, once more united to his brave wounded companions under that roof which covers a household of as noble hearts as ever throbbed with human sympathies. Back River, Bush River, Gunpowder Creek,—lives there the man with soul so dead that his memory has cerements to wrap up these senseless names in the same envelopes with their meaningless localities? But the Susquehanna,—the broad, the beautiful, the historical, the poetical Susquehanna,—the river of Wyoming and of Gertrude, dividing the shores where did not my heart renew its allegiance to the poet who has made it lovely to the imagination as well as to the eye, and so identified his fame with the noble stream that it "rolls mingling with his fame forever?" The prosaic traveller perhaps remembers it better from the fact that a great sea-monster, in the shape of a steamboat, takes him, sitting in the car, on its back, and swims across with him like Arion's dolphin,—also that mercenary men on board offer him canvas-backs in the season, and ducks of lower degree at other periods.

At Philadelphia again at last! Drive fast, O colored man and brother, to the house called Beautiful, where my Captain lies sore wounded, waiting for the sound of the chariot wheels which bring to his bedside the face and the voice nearer than any save one to his heart in this his hour of pain and weakness! Up a long street with white shutters and white steps to all the houses. Off at right angles into another long street with white shutters and white steps to all the houses. Off again at another right angle into still another long street with white shutters and white steps to all the houses. The natives of this city pretend to know one street from another by some individual differences of aspect; but the best way for a stranger to distinguish the streets he has been in from others is to make a cross or other mark on the white shutters.

This corner-house is the one. Ring softly,—for the Lieutenant-Colonel lies there with a dreadfully wounded arm, and two sons of the family, one wounded like the Colonel, one fighting with death in the fog of a typhoid fever, will start with fresh pangs at the least sound you can make. I entered the house, but no cheerful smile met me. The sufferers were each of them thought to be in a critical condition. The fourth bed, waiting its tenant day after day, was still empty. Not a word from my Captain.

Then, foolish, fond body that I was, my heart sank within me. Had he been taken ill on the road, perhaps been attacked with those formidable symptoms which sometimes come on suddenly after wounds that seemed to be doing well enough, and was his life ebbing away in some lonely cottage, nay, in some cold barn or shed, or at the wayside, unknown, uncared for? Somewhere between Philadelphia and Hagerstown, if not at the latter town, he must be, at any rate. I must sweep the hundred and eighty miles between these places as one would sweep a chamber where a precious pearl had been dropped. I must have a companion in my search, partly to help me look about, and partly because I was getting nervous and felt lonely. Charley said he would go with me,—Charley, my Captain's beloved friend, gentle, but full of spirit and liveliness, cultivated, social, affectionate, a good talker, a most agreeable letter-writer, observing, with large relish of life, and keen sense of humor. He was not well enough to go, some of the timid ones said; but he answered by packing his carpet-bag, and in an hour or two we were on the Pennsylvania Central Railroad in full blast for Harrisburg.

I should have been a forlorn creature but for the presence of my companion. In his delightful company I half forgot my anxieties, which, exaggerated as they may seem now, were not unnatural after what I had seen of the confusion and distress that had followed the great battle, nay, which seem almost justified by the recent statement that "high officers" were buried after that battle whose names were never ascertained. I noticed little matters, as usual. The road was filled in between the rails with cracked stones, such as are used for macadamizing streets. They keep the dust down, I suppose, for I could not think of any other use for them. By and by the glorious valley which stretches along through Chester and Lancaster Counties opened upon us. Much as I had heard of the fertile regions of Pennsylvania, the vast scale and the uniform luxuriance of this region astonished me. The grazing pastures were so green, the fields were under such perfect culture, the cattle looked so sleek, the houses were so comfortable, the barns so ample, the fences so well kept, that I did not wonder, when I was told that this region was called the England of Pennsylvania. The people whom we saw were, like the cattle, well nourished; the young women looked round and wholesome.

"Grass makes girls." I said to my companion, and left him to work out my Orphic saying, thinking to myself, that as guano makes grass, it was a legitimate conclusion that Ichaboe must be a nursery of female loveliness.

As the train stopped at the different stations, I inquired at each if they had any wounded officers. None as yet; the red rays of the battle-field had not streamed off so far as this. Evening found us in the cars; they lighted candles in spring-candle-sticks; odd enough I thought it in the land of oil-wells and unmeasured floods of kerosene. Some fellows turned up the back of a seat so as to make it horizontal, and began gambling, or pretending to gamble; it looked as if they were trying to pluck a young countryman; but appearances are deceptive, and no deeper stake than "drinks for the crowd" seemed at last to be involved. But remembering that murder has tried of late years to establish itself as an institution in the cars, I was less tolerant of the doings of these "sportsmen" who tried to turn our public conveyance into a travelling Frascati. They acted as if they were used to it, and nobody seemed to pay much attention to their manoeuvres.

We arrived at Harrisburg in the course of the evening, and attempted to find our way to the Jones House, to which we had been commended. By some mistake, intentional on the part of somebody, as it may have been, or purely accidental, we went to the Herr House instead. I entered my name in the book, with that of my companion. A plain, middle-aged man stepped up, read it to himself in low tones, and coupled to it a literary title by which I have been sometimes known. He proved to be a graduate of Brown University, and had heard a certain Phi Beta Kappa poem delivered there a good many years ago. I remembered it, too; Professor Goddard, whose sudden and singular death left such lasting regret, was the Orator. I recollect that while I was speaking a drum went by the church, and how I was disgusted to see all the heads near the windows thrust out of them, as if the building were on fire. Cedat armis toga. The clerk in the office, a mild, pensive, unassuming young man, was very polite in his manners, and did all he could to make us comfortable. He was of a literary turn, and knew one of his guests in his character of author. At tea, a mild old gentleman, with white hair and beard, sat next us. He, too, had come hunting after his son, a lieutenant in a Pennsylvania regiment. Of these, father and son, more presently.

After tea we went to look up Dr. Wilson, chief medical officer of the hospitals in the place, who was staying at the Brady House. A magnificent old toddy-mixer, Bardolphian in hue, and stern of aspect, as all grog-dispensers must be, accustomed as they are to dive through the features of men to the bottom of their souls and pockets to see whether they are solvent to the amount of sixpence, answered my question by a wave of one hand, the other being engaged in carrying a dram to his lips. His superb indifference gratified my artistic feeling more than it wounded my personal sensibilities. Anything really superior in its line claims my homage, and this man was the ideal bartender, above all vulgar passions, untouched by commonplace sympathies, himself a lover of the liquid happiness he dispenses, and filled with a fine scorn of all those lesser felicities conferred by love or fame or wealth or any of the roundabout agencies for which his fiery elixir is the cheap, all-powerful substitute.

Dr. Wilson was in bed, though it was early in the evening, not having slept for I don't know how many nights.

"Take my card up to him, if you please."

"This way, sir."

A man who has not slept for a fortnight or so is not expected to be as affable, when attacked in his bed, as a French Princess of old time at her morning receptions. Dr. Wilson turned toward me, as I entered, without effusion, but without rudeness. His thick, dark moustache was chopped off square at the lower edge of the upper lip, which implied a decisive, if not a peremptory, style of character.

I am Dr. So-and-So of Hubtown, looking after my wounded son. (I gave my name and said Boston, of course, in reality.)

Dr. Wilson leaned on his elbow and looked up in my face, his features growing cordial. Then he put out his hand, and good-humoredly excused his reception of me. The day before, as he told me, he had dismissed from the service a medical man hailing from ******, Pennsylvania, bearing my last name, preceded by the same two initials; and he supposed, when my card came up, it was this individual who was disturbing his slumbers. The coincidence was so unlikely a priori, unless some forlorn parent without antecedents had named, a child after me, that I could not help cross-questioning the Doctor, who assured me deliberately that the fact was just as he had said, even to the somewhat unusual initials. Dr. Wilson very kindly furnished me all the information in his power, gave me directions for telegraphing to Chambersburg, and showed every disposition to serve me.

On returning to the Herr House, we found the mild, white-haired old gentleman in a very happy state. He had just discovered his son, in a comfortable condition, at the United States Hotel. He thought that he could probably give us some information which would prove interesting. To the United States Hotel we repaired, then, in company with our kind-hearted old friend, who evidently wanted to see me as happy as himself. He went up-stairs to his son's chamber, and presently came down to conduct us there.

Lieutenant P________, of the Pennsylvania __th, was a very fresh, bright-looking young man, lying in bed from the effects of a recent injury received in action. A grape-shot, after passing through a post and a board, had struck him in the hip, bruising, but not penetrating or breaking. He had good news for me.

That very afternoon, a party of wounded officers had passed through Harrisburg, going East. He had conversed in the bar-room of this hotel with one of them, who was wounded about the shoulder (it might be the lower part of the neck), and had his arm in a sling. He belonged to the Twentieth Massachusetts; the Lieutenant saw that he was a Captain, by the two bars on his shoulder-strap. His name was my family name; he was tall and youthful, like my Captain. At four o'clock he left in the train for Philadelphia. Closely questioned, the Lieutenant's evidence was as round, complete, and lucid as a Japanese sphere of rock-crystal.

TE DEUM LAUDAMUS! The Lord's name be praised! The dead pain in the semilunar ganglion (which I must remind my reader is a kind of stupid, unreasoning brain, beneath the pit of the stomach, common to man and beast, which aches in the supreme moments of life, as when the dam loses her young ones, or the wild horse is lassoed) stopped short. There was a feeling as if I had slipped off a tight boot, or cut a strangling garter,—only it was all over my system. What more could I ask to assure me of the Captain's safety? As soon as the telegraph office opens tomorrow morning we will send a message to our friends in Philadelphia, and get a reply, doubtless, which will settle the whole matter.

The hopeful morrow dawned at last, and the message was sent accordingly. In due time, the following reply was received: "Phil Sept 24 I think the report you have heard that W [the Captain] has gone East must be an error we have not seen or heard of him here M L H."

DE PROFUNDIS CLAMAVI! He could not have passed through Philadelphia without visiting the house called Beautiful, where he had been so tenderly cared for after his wound at Ball's Bluff, and where those whom he loved were lying in grave peril of life or limb. Yet he did pass through Harrisburg, going East, going to Philadelphia, on his way home. Ah, this is it! He must have taken the late night-train from Philadelphia for New York, in his impatience to reach home. There is such a train, not down in the guide-book, but we were assured of the fact at the Harrisburg depot. By and by came the reply from Dr. Wilson's telegraphic message: nothing had been heard of the Captain at Chambersburg. Still later, another message came from our Philadelphia friend, saying that he was seen on Friday last at the house of Mrs. K______, a well-known Union lady in Hagerstown. Now this could not be true, for he did not leave Keedysville until Saturday; but the name of the lady furnished a clew by which we could probably track him. A telegram was at once sent to Mrs. K______, asking information. It was transmitted immediately, but when the answer would be received was uncertain, as the Government almost monopolized the line. I was, on the whole, so well satisfied that the Captain had gone East, that, unless something were heard to the contrary, I proposed following him in the late train leaving a little after midnight for Philadelphia.

This same morning we visited several of the temporary hospitals, churches and school-houses, where the wounded were lying. In one of these, after looking round as usual, I asked aloud, "Any Massachusetts men here?" Two bright faces lifted themselves from their pillows and welcomed me by name. The one nearest me was private John B. Noyes of Company

B, Massachusetts Thirteenth, son of my old college class-tutor, now the reverend and learned Professor of Hebrew, etc., in Harvard University. His neighbor was Corporal Armstrong of the same Company. Both were slightly wounded, doing well. I learned then and since from Mr. Noyes that they and their comrades were completely overwhelmed by the attentions of the good people of Harrisburg,—that the ladies brought them fruits and flowers, and smiles, better than either,—and that the little boys of the place were almost fighting for the privilege of doing their errands. I am afraid there will be a good many hearts pierced in this war that will have no bulletmark to show.

There were some heavy hours to get rid of, and we thought a visit to Camp Curtin might lighten some of them. A rickety wagon carried us to the camp, in company with a young woman from Troy, who had a basket of good things with her for a sick brother. "Poor boy! he will be sure to die," she said. The rustic sentries uncrossed their muskets and let us in. The camp was on a fair plain, girdled with hills, spacious, well kept apparently, but did not present any peculiar attraction for us. The visit would have been a dull one, had we not happened to get sight of a singular-looking set of human beings in the distance. They were clad in stuff of different hues, gray and brown being the leading shades, but both subdued by a neutral tint, such as is wont to harmonize the variegated apparel of travel-stained vagabonds. They looked slouchy, listless, torpid,—an ill-conditioned crew, at first sight, made up of such fellows as an old woman would drive away from her hen-roost with a broomstick. Yet these were estrays from the fiery army which has given our generals so much trouble,—"Secesh prisoners," as a bystander told us. A talk with them might be profitable and entertaining. But they were tabooed to the common visitor, and it was necessary to get inside of the line which separated us from them.

A solid, square captain was standing near by, to whom we were referred. Look a man calmly through the very centre of his pupils and ask him for anything with a tone implying entire conviction that he will grant it, and he will very commonly consent to the thing asked, were it to commit hari-kari. The Captain acceded to my postulate, and accepted my friend as a corollary. As one string of my own ancestors was of Batavian origin, I may be permitted to say that my new friend was of the Dutch type, like the Amsterdam galiots, broad in the beam, capacious in the hold, and calculated to carry a heavy cargo rather than to make fast time. He must have been in politics at some time or other, for he made orations to all the "Secesh," in which he explained to them that the United States considered and treated them like children, and enforced upon them the ridiculous impossibility of the Rebels attempting to do anything against such a power as that of the National Government.

Much as his discourse edified them and enlightened me, it interfered somewhat with my little plans of entering into frank and friendly talk with some of these poor fellows, for whom I could not help feeling a kind of human sympathy, though I am as venomous a hater of the Rebellion as one is like to find under the stars and stripes. It is fair to take a man prisoner. It is fair to make speeches to a man. But to take a man prisoner and then make speeches to him while in durance is not fair.

I began a few pleasant conversations, which would have come to something but for the reason assigned.

One old fellow had a long beard, a drooping eyelid, and a black clay pipe in his mouth. He was a Scotchman from Ayr, dour enough, and little disposed to be communicative, though I tried him with the "Twa Briggs," and, like all Scotchmen, he was a reader of "Burrns." He professed to feel no interest in the cause for which he was fighting, and was in the army, I judged, only from compulsion. There was a wild-haired, unsoaped boy, with pretty, foolish features enough, who looked as if he might be about seventeen, as he said he was. I give my questions and his answers literally.

"What State do you come from?"

"Georgy."

"What part of Georgia?"

"Midway."

—[How odd that is! My father was settled for seven years as pastor over the church at Midway, Georgia, and this youth is very probably a grandson or great grandson of one of his parishioners.]

"Where did you go to church when you were at home?"

"Never went inside 'f a church b't once in m' life."

"What did you do before you became a soldier?"

"Nothin'."

"What do you mean to do when you get back?"

"Nothin'."

Who could have any other feeling than pity for this poor human weed, this dwarfed and etiolated soul, doomed by neglect to an existence but one degree above that of the idiot?

With the group was a lieutenant, buttoned close in his gray coat,—one button gone, perhaps to make a breastpin for some fair traitorous bosom. A short, stocky man, undistinguishable from one of the "subject race" by any obvious meanderings of the sangre azul on his exposed surfaces. He did not say much, possibly because he was convinced by the statements and arguments of the Dutch captain. He had on strong, iron-heeled shoes, of English make, which he said cost him seventeen dollars in Richmond.

I put the question, in a quiet, friendly way, to several of the prisoners, what they were fighting for. One answered, "For our homes." Two or three others said they did not know, and manifested great indifference to the whole matter, at which another of their number, a sturdy fellow, took offence, and muttered opinions strongly derogatory to those who would not stand up for the cause they had been fighting for. A feeble; attenuated old man, who wore the Rebel uniform, if such it could be called, stood by without showing any sign of intelligence. It was cutting very close to the bone to carve such a shred of humanity from the body politic to make a soldier of.

We were just leaving, when a face attracted me, and I stopped the party. "That is the true Southern type," I said to my companion. A young fellow, a little over twenty, rather tall, slight, with a perfectly smooth, boyish cheek, delicate, somewhat high features, and a fine, almost feminine mouth, stood at the opening of his tent, and as we turned towards him fidgeted a little nervously with one hand at the loose canvas, while he seemed at the same time not unwilling to talk. He was from Mississippi, he said, had been at Georgetown College, and was so far imbued with letters that even the name of the literary humility before him was not new to his ears. Of course I found it easy to come into magnetic relation with him, and to ask him without incivility what he was fighting for. "Because I like the excitement of it," he answered. I know those fighters with women's mouths and boys' cheeks. One such from the circle of my own friends, sixteen years old, slipped away from his nursery, and dashed in under, an assumed name among the red-legged Zouaves, in whose company he got an ornamental bullet-mark in one of the earliest conflicts of the war.

"Did you ever see a genuine Yankee?" said my Philadelphia friend to the young Mississippian.

"I have shot at a good many of them," he replied, modestly, his woman's mouth stirring a little, with a pleasant, dangerous smile.

The Dutch captain here put his foot into the conversation, as his ancestors used to put theirs into the scale, when they were buying furs of the Indians by weight,—so much for the weight of a hand, so much for the weight of a foot. It deranged the balance of our intercourse; there was no use in throwing a fly where a paving-stone had just splashed into the water, and I nodded a good-by to the boy-fighter, thinking how much pleasanter it was for my friend the Captain to address him with unanswerable arguments and crushing statements in his own tent than it would be to meet him upon some remote picket station and offer his fair proportions to the quick eye of a youngster who would draw a bead on him before he had time to say dunder and blixum.

We drove back to the town. No message. After dinner still no message. Dr. Cuyler, Chief Army Hospital Inspector, is in town, they say. Let us hunt him up, — perhaps he can help us.

We found him at the Jones House. A gentleman of large proportions, but of lively temperament, his frame knit in the North, I think, but ripened in Georgia, incisive, prompt but good-humored, wearing his broad-brimmed, steeple-crowned felt hat with the least possible tilt on one side, — a sure sign of exuberant vitality in a mature and dignified person like him, business-like in his ways, and not to be interrupted while occupied with another, but giving himself up heartily to the claimant who held him for the time. He was so genial, so cordial, so encouraging, that it seemed as if the clouds, which had been thick all the morning, broke away as we came into his presence, and the sunshine of his large nature filled the air all around us. He took the matter in hand at once, as if it were his own private affair. In ten minutes he had a second telegraphic message on its way to Mrs. K at Hagerstown, sent through the Government channel from the State Capitol, — one so direct and urgent that I should be sure of an answer to it, whatever became of the one I had sent in the morning.

While this was going on, we hired a dilapidated barouche, driven by an odd young native, neither boy nor man, "as a codling when 't is almost an apple," who said wery for very, simple and sincere, who smiled faintly at our pleasantries, always with a certain reserve of suspicion, and a gleam of the shrewdness that all men get who live in the atmosphere of horses. He drove us round by the Capitol grounds, white with tents, which were disgraced in my eyes by unsoldierly scrawls in huge letters, thus: THE SEVEN BLOOMSBURY BROTHERS, DEVIL'S HOLE, and similar inscriptions. Then to the Beacon Street of Harrisburg, which looks upon the Susquehanna instead of the Common, and shows a long front of handsome houses with fair gardens. The river is pretty nearly a mile across here, but very shallow now. The codling told us that a Rebel spy had been caught trying its fords a little while ago, and was now at Camp Curtin with a heavy ball chained to his leg, — a popular story, but a lie, Dr. Wilson said. A little farther along we came to the barkless stump of the tree to which Mr. Harris, the Cecrops of the city named after him, was tied by the Indians for some unpleasant operation of scalping or roasting, when he was rescued by friendly savages, who paddled across the stream to save him. Our youngling pointed out a very respectable-looking stone house as having been "built by the Indians" about those times. Guides have queer notions occasionally.

I was at Niagara just when Dr. Rae arrived there with his companions and dogs and things from his Arctic search after the lost navigator.

"Who are those?" I said to my conductor.

"Them?" he answered. "Them's the men that's been out West, out to Michig'n, aft' Sir Ben Franklin."

Of the other sights of Harrisburg the Brant House or Hotel, or whatever it is called, seems most worth notice. Its facade is imposing, with a row of stately columns, high above which a broad sign impends, like a crag over the brow of a lofty precipice. The lower floor only appeared to be open to the public. Its tessellated pavement and ample courts suggested the idea of a temple where great multitudes might kneel uncrowded at their devotions; but from appearances about the place where the altar should be, I judged, that, if one asked the officiating priest for the cup which cheers and likewise inebriates, his prayer would not be unanswered. The edifice recalled to me a similar phenomenon I had once looked upon,—the famous Caffe Pedrocchi at Padua. It was the same thing in Italy and America: a rich man builds himself a mausoleum, and calls it a place of entertainment. The fragrance of innumerable libations and the smoke of incense-breathing cigars and pipes shall ascend day and night through the arches of his funereal monument. What are the poor dips which flare and flicker on the crowns of spikes that stand at the corners of St. Genevieve's filigree-cased sarcophagus to this perpetual offering of sacrifice?

Ten o'clock in the evening was approaching. The telegraph office would presently close, and as yet there were no tidings from Hagerstown. Let us step over and see for ourselves. A message! A message!

"Captain H. still here leaves seven to-morrow for Harrisburg Penna Is doing well Mrs HK—."

A note from Dr. Cuyler to the same effect came soon afterwards to the hotel.

We shall sleep well to-night; but let us sit awhile with nubiferous, or, if we may coin a word, nepheligenous accompaniment, such as shall gently narcotize the over wearied brain and fold its convolutions for slumber like the leaves of a lily at nightfall. For now the over-tense nerves are all unstraining themselves, and a buzz, like that which comes over one who stops after being long jolted upon an uneasy pavement, makes the whole frame alive with a luxurious languid sense of all its inmost fibres. Our cheerfulness ran over, and the mild, pensive clerk was so magnetized by it that he came and sat down with us. He presently confided to me, with infinite naivete and ingenuousness, that, judging from my personal appearance, he should not have thought me the writer that he in his generosity reckoned me to be. His conception, so far as I could reach it, involved a huge, uplifted forehead, embossed with protuberant organs of the intellectual faculties, such as all writers are supposed to possess in abounding measure. While I fell short of his ideal in this respect, he was pleased to say that he found me by no means the remote and inaccessible personage he had imagined, and that I had nothing of the dandy about me, which last compliment I had a modest consciousness of most abundantly deserving.

Sweet slumbers brought us to the morning of Thursday. The train from Hagerstown was due at 11.15 A. M: We took another ride behind the codling, who showed us the sights of yesterday over again. Being in a gracious mood of mind, I enlarged on the varying aspects of the town-pumps and other striking objects which we had once inspected, as seen by the different lights of evening and morning. After this, we visited the school-house hospital. A fine young fellow, whose arm had been shattered, was just falling into the spasms of lock-jaw. The beads of sweat stood large and round on his flushed and contracted features. He was under the effect of opiates, — why not (if his case was desperate, as it seemed to be considered) stop his sufferings with chloroform? It was suggested that it might shorten life. "What then?" I said. "Are a dozen additional spasms worth living for?"

The time approached for the train to arrive from Hagerstown, and we went to the station. I was struck, while waiting there, with what seemed to me a great want of care for the safety of the people standing round. Just after my companion and myself had stepped off the track, I noticed a car coming quietly along at a walk, as one may say, without engine, without visible conductor, without any person heralding its approach, so silently, so insidiously, that I could not help thinking how very near it came to flattening out me and my match-box worse than the Ravel pantomimist and his snuff-box were flattened out in the play. The train was late, — fifteen minutes, half an hour late, and I began to get nervous, lest something had happened. While I was looking for it, out started a freight-train, as if on purpose to meet the cars I was expecting, for a grand smash-up. I shivered at the thought, and asked an employee of the road, with whom I had formed an acquaintance a few minutes old, why there should not be a collision of the expected train with this which was just going out. He smiled an official smile, and answered that they arranged to prevent that, or words to that effect.

Twenty-four hours had not passed from that moment when a collision did occur, just out of the city, where I feared it, by which at least eleven persons were killed, and from forty to sixty more were maimed and crippled!

To-day there was the delay spoken of, but nothing worse. The expected train came in so quietly that I was almost startled to see it on the track. Let us walk calmly through the cars, and look around us.

In the first car, on the fourth seat to the right, I saw my Captain; there saw I him, even my first-born, whom I had sought through many cities.

"How are you, Boy?"

"How are you, Dad?"

Such are the proprieties of life, as they are observed among us Anglo-Saxons of the nineteenth century, decently disguising those natural impulses that made Joseph, the Prime Minister of Egypt, weep aloud so that the Egyptians and the house of Pharaoh heard, nay, which had once overcome his shaggy old uncle Esau so entirely that he fell on his brother's neck and cried like a baby in the presence of all the women. But the hidden cisterns of the soul may be filling fast with sweet tears, while the windows through which it looks are undimmed by a drop or a film of moisture.

These are times in which we cannot live solely for selfish joys or griefs. I had not let fall the hand I held, when a sad, calm voice addressed me by name. I fear that at the moment I was too much absorbed in my own feelings; for certainly at any other time. I should have yielded myself without stint to the sympathy which this meeting might well call forth.

"You remember my son, Cortland Saunders, whom I brought to see you once in Boston?"

"I do remember him well."

"He was killed on Monday, at Shepherdstown. I am carrying his body back with me on this train. He was my only child. If you could come to my house, — I can hardly call it my home now, — it would be a pleasure to me."

This young man, belonging in Philadelphia, was the author of a "New System of Latin Paradigms," a work showing extraordinary scholarship and capacity. It was this book which first made me acquainted with him, and I kept him in my memory, for there was genius in the youth. Some time afterwards he came to me with a modest request to be introduced to President Felton, and one or two others, who would aid him in a course of independent study he was proposing to himself. I was most happy to smooth the way for him, and he came repeatedly after this to see me and express his satisfaction in the opportunities for study he enjoyed at Cambridge. He was a dark, still, slender person, always with a trance-like remoteness, a mystic dreaminess of manner, such as I never saw in any other youth. Whether he heard with difficulty, or whether his mind reacted slowly on an alien thought, I could not say; but his answer would often be behind time, and then a vague, sweet smile, or a few words spoken under his breath, as if he had been trained in sick men's chambers. For such a young man, seemingly destined for the inner life of contemplation, to be a soldier seemed almost unnatural. Yet he spoke to me of his intention to offer himself to his country, and his blood must now be reckoned among the precious sacrifices which will make her soil sacred forever. Had he lived, I doubt not that he would have redeemed the rare promise of his earlier years. He has done better, for he has died that unborn generations may attain the hopes held out to our nation and to mankind.

So, then, I had been within ten miles of the place where my wounded soldier was lying, and then calmly turned my back upon him to come once more round by a journey of three or four hundred miles to the same region I had left! No mysterious attraction warned me that the heart warm with the same blood as mine was throbbing so near my own. I thought of that lovely, tender passage where Gabriel glides unconsciously by Evangeline upon the great river. Ah, me! if that railroad crash had been a few hours earlier, we two should never have met again, after coming so close to each other!

The source of my repeated disappointments was soon made clear enough. The Captain had gone to Hagerstown, intending to take the cars at once for Philadelphia, as his three friends actually did, and as I took it for granted he certainly would. But as he walked languidly along, some ladies saw him across the street, and seeing, were moved with pity, and pitying, spoke such soft words that he was tempted to accept their invitation and rest awhile beneath their hospitable roof. The mansion was old, as the dwellings of gentlefolks should be; the ladies were some of them young, and all were full of kindness; there were gentle cares, and unasked luxuries, and pleasant talk, and music-sprinklings from the piano, with a sweet voice to keep them company,—and all this after the swamps of the Chickahominy, the mud and flies of Harrison's Landing, the dragging marches, the desperate battles, the fretting wound, the jolting ambulance, the log-house, and the rickety milk—cart! Thanks, uncounted thanks to the angelic ladies whose charming attentions detained him from Saturday to Thursday, to his great advantage and my infinite bewilderment! As for his wound, how could it do otherwise than well under such hands? The bullet had gone smoothly through, dodging everything but a few nervous branches, which would come right in time and leave him as well as ever.

At ten that evening we were in Philadelphia, the Captain at the house of the friends so often referred to, and I the guest of Charley, my kind companion. The Quaker element gives an irresistible attraction to these benignant Philadelphia households. Many things reminded me that I was no longer in the land of the Pilgrims. On the table were Kool Slaa and Schmeer Kase, but the good grandmother who dispensed with such quiet, simple grace these and more familiar delicacies was literally ignorant of Baked Beans, and asked if it was the Lima bean which was employed in that marvellous dish of animalized leguminous farina!

Charley was pleased with my comparing the face of the small Ethiop known to his household as "Tines" to a huckleberry with features. He also approved my parallel between a certain German blonde young maiden whom we passed in the street and the "Morris White" peach. But he was so good-humored at times, that, if one scratched a lucifer, he accepted it as an illumination.

A day in Philadelphia left a very agreeable impression of the outside of that great city, which has endeared itself so much of late to all the country by its most noble and generous care of our soldiers. Measured by its sovereign hotel, the Continental, it would stand at the head of our economic civilization. It provides for the comforts and conveniences, and many of the elegances of life, more satisfactorily than any American city, perhaps than any other city anywhere. Many of its characteristics are accounted for to some extent by its geographical position. It is the great neutral centre of the Continent, where the fiery enthusiasms of the South and the keen fanaticisms of the North meet at their outer limits, and result in a compound which neither turns litmus red nor turmeric brown. It lives largely on its traditions, of which, leaving out Franklin and Independence Hall, the most imposing must be considered its famous water-works. In my younger days I visited Fairmount, and it was with a pious reverence that I renewed my pilgrimage to that perennial fountain. Its watery ventricles were throbbing with the same systole and diastole as when, the blood of twenty years bounding in my own heart, I looked upon their giant mechanism. But in the place of "Pratt's Garden" was an open park, and the old house where Robert Morris held his court in a former generation was changing to a public restaurant. A suspension bridge cobwebbed itself across the Schuylkill where that audacious arch used to leap the river at a single bound,—an arch of greater span, as they loved to tell us, than was ever before constructed. The Upper Ferry Bridge was to the Schuylkill what the Colossus was to the harbor of Rhodes. It had an air of dash about it which went far towards redeeming the dead level of respectable average which flattens the physiognomy of the rectangular city. Philadelphia will never be herself again until another Robert Mills and another Lewis Wernwag have shaped her a new palladium. She must leap the Schuylkill again, or old men will sadly shake their heads, like the Jews at the sight of the second temple, remembering the glories of that which it replaced.

There are times when Ethiopian minstrelsy can amuse, if it does not charm, a weary soul, and such a vacant hour there was on this same Friday evening. The "opera-house" was spacious and admirably ventilated. As I was listening to the merriment of the sooty buffoons, I happened to cast my eyes up to the ceiling, and through an open semicircular window a bright solitary star looked me calmly in the eyes. It was a strange intrusion of the vast eternities beckoning from the infinite spaces. I called the attention of one of my neighbors to it, but "Bones" was irresistibly droll, and Arcturus, or Aldebaran, or whatever the blazing luminary may have been, with all his revolving worlds, sailed uncared-for down the firmament.

On Saturday morning we took up our line of march for New York. Mr. Felton, President of the Philadelphia, Wilmington and Baltimore Railroad, had already called upon me, with a benevolent and sagacious look on his face which implied that he knew how to do me a service and meant to do it. Sure enough, when we got to the depot, we found a couch spread for the Captain, and both of us were passed on to New York with no visits, but those of civility, from the conductor. The best thing I saw on the route was a rustic fence, near Elizabethtown, I think, but I am not quite sure. There was more genius in it than in any structure of the kind I have ever seen,— each length being of a special pattern, ramified, reticulated, contorted, as the limbs of the trees had grown. I trust some friend will photograph or stereograph this fence for me, to go with the view of the spires of Frederick, already referred to, as mementos of my journey.

I had come to feeling that I knew most of the respectably dressed people whom I met in the cars, and had been in contact with them at some time or other. Three or four ladies and gentlemen were near us, forming a group by themselves. Presently one addressed me by name, and, on inquiry, I found him to be the gentleman who was with me in the pulpit as Orator on the occasion of another Phi Beta Kappa poem, one delivered at New Haven. The party were very courteous and friendly, and contributed in various ways to our comfort.

It sometimes seems to me as if there were only about a thousand people in the world, who keep going round and round behind the scenes and then before them, like the "army" in a beggarly stage-show. Suppose that I should really wish, some time or other, to get away from this everlasting circle of revolving supernumeraries, where should I buy a ticket the like of which was not in some of their pockets, or find a seat to which some one of them was not a neighbor.

A little less than a year before, after the Ball's Bluff accident, the Captain, then the Lieutenant, and myself had reposed for a night on our homeward journey at the Fifth Avenue Hotel, where we were lodged on the ground-floor, and fared sumptuously. We were not so peculiarly fortunate this time, the house being really very full. Farther from the flowers and nearer to the stars,—to reach the neighborhood of which last the per ardua of three or four flights of stairs was formidable for any mortal, wounded or well.

The "vertical railway" settled that for us, however. It is a giant corkscrew forever pulling a mammoth cork, which, by some divine judgment, is no sooner drawn than it is replaced in its position. This ascending and descending stopper is hollow, carpeted, with cushioned seats, and is watched over by two condemned souls, called conductors, one of whom is said to be named Igion, and the other Sisyphus.

I love New York, because, as in Paris, everybody that lives in it feels that it is his property,—at least, as much as it is anybody's. My Broadway, in particular, I love almost as I used to love my Boulevards. I went, therefore, with peculiar interest, on the day that we rested at our grand hotel, to visit some new pleasure-grounds the citizens had been arranging for us, and which I had not yet seen. The Central Park is an expanse of wild country, well crumpled so as to form ridges which will give views and hollows that will hold water. The hips and elbows and other bones of Nature stick out here and there in the shape of rocks which give character to the scenery, and an unchangeable, unpurchasable look to a landscape that without them would have been in danger of being fattened by art and money out of all its native features. The roads were fine, the sheets of water beautiful, the bridges handsome, the swans elegant in their deportment, the grass green and as short as a fast horse's winter coat. I could not learn whether it was kept so by clipping or singeing. I was delighted with my new property,— but it cost me four dollars to get there, so far was it beyond the Pillars of Hercules of the fashionable quarter. What it will be by and by depends on circumstances; but at present it is as much central to New York as Brookline is central to Boston.

The question is not between Mr. Olmsted's admirably arranged, but remote pleasure-ground and our Common, with its batrachian pool, but between his Excentric Park and our finest suburban scenery, between its artificial reservoirs and the broad natural sheet of Jamaica Pond. I say this not invidiously, but in justice to the beauties which surround our own metropolis. To compare the situations of any dwellings in either of the great cities with those which look upon the Common, the Public Garden, the waters of the Back Bay, would be to take an unfair advantage of Fifth Avenue and Walnut Street. St. Botolph's daughter dresses in plainer clothes than her more stately sisters, but she wears an emerald on her right hand and a diamond on her left that Cybele herself need not be ashamed of.

On Monday morning, the twenty-ninth of September, we took the cars for home. Vacant lots, with Irish and pigs; vegetable-gardens; straggling houses; the high bridge; villages, not enchanting; then Stamford: then NORWALK. Here, on the sixth of May, 1853, I passed close on the heels of the great disaster. But that my lids were heavy on that morning, my readers would probably have had no further trouble with me. Two of my friends saw the car in which they rode break in the middle and leave them hanging over the abyss. From Norwalk to Boston, that day's journey of two hundred miles was a long funeral procession.

Bridgeport, waiting for Iranistan to rise from its ashes with all its phoenix-egg domes,—bubbles of wealth that broke, ready to be blown again; iridescent as ever, which is pleasant, for the world likes cheerful Mr. Barnum's success; New Haven, girt with flat marshes that look like monstrous billiard-tables, with hay-cocks lying about for balls,—romantic with West Rock and its legends,—cursed with a detestable depot, whose niggardly arrangements crowd the track so murderously close to the wall that the peine forte et dare must be the frequent penalty of an innocent walk on its platform,—with its neat carriages, metropolitan hotels, precious old college-dormitories, its vistas of elms and its dishevelled weeping-willows; Hartford, substantial, well-bridged, many—steepled city,—every conical spire an extinguisher of some nineteenth-century heresy; so onward, by and across the broad, shallow Connecticut,—dull red road and dark river woven in like warp and woof by the shuttle of the darting engine; then Springfield, the wide-meadowed, well-feeding, horse-loving, hot-summered, giant-treed town,—city among villages, village among cities; Worcester, with its Daedalian labyrinth of crossing railroad-bars, where the snorting Minotaurs, breathing fire and smoke and hot vapors, are stabled in their dens; Framingham, fair cup-bearer, leaf-cinctured Hebe of the deep-bosomed Queen sitting by the seaside on the throne of the Six Nations. And now I begin to know the road, not by towns, but by single dwellings; not by miles, but by rods. The poles of the great magnet that draws in all the iron tracks through the grooves of all the mountains must be near at hand, for here are crossings, and sudden stops, and screams of alarmed engines heard all around. The tall granite obelisk comes into view far away on the left, its bevelled cap-stone sharp against the sky; the lofty chimneys of

Charlestown and East Cambridge flaunt their smoky banners up in the thin air; and now one fair bosom of the three-pilled city, with its dome-crowned summit, reveals itself, as when many-breasted Ephesian Artemis appeared with half-open chlamys before her worshippers.

Fling open the window-blinds of the chamber that looks out on the waters and towards the western sun! Let the joyous light shine in upon the pictures that hang upon its walls and the shelves thick-set with the names of poets and philosophers and sacred teachers, in whose pages our boys learn that life is noble only when it is held cheap by the side of honor and of duty. Lay him in his own bed, and let him sleep off his aches and weariness. So comes down another night over this household, unbroken by any messenger of evil tidings,—a night of peaceful rest and grateful thoughts; for this our son and brother was dead and is alive again, and was lost and is found.

THE INEVITABLE TRIAL

[An Oration delivered before the City Authorities of Boston, on the 4th of July, 1863.]

It is our first impulse, upon this returning day of our nation's birth, to recall whatever is happiest and noblest in our past history, and to join our voices in celebrating the statesmen and the heroes, the men of thought and the men of action, to whom that history owes its existence. In other years this pleasing office may have been all that was required of the holiday speaker. But to-day, when the very life of the nation is threatened, when clouds are thick about us, and men's hearts are throbbing with passion, or failing with fear, it is the living question of the hour, and not the dead story of the past, which forces itself into all minds, and will find unrebuked debate in all assemblies.

In periods of disturbance like the present, many persons who sincerely love their country and mean to do their duty to her disappoint the hopes and expectations of those who are actively working in her cause. They seem to have lost whatever moral force they may have once possessed, and to go drifting about from one profitless discontent to another, at a time when every citizen is called upon for cheerful, ready service. It is because their minds are bewildered, and they are no longer truly themselves. Show them the path of duty, inspire them with hope for the future, lead them upwards from the turbid stream of events to the bright, translucent springs of eternal principles, strengthen their trust in humanity and their faith in God, and you may yet restore them to their manhood and their country.

At all times, and especially on this anniversary of glorious recollections and kindly enthusiasms, we should try to judge the weak and wavering souls of our brothers fairly and generously. The conditions in which our vast community of peace-loving citizens find themselves are new and unprovided for. Our quiet burghers and farmers are in the position of river-boats blown from their moorings out upon a vast ocean, where such a typhoon is raging as no mariner who sails its waters ever before looked upon. If their beliefs change with the veering of the blast, if their trust in their fellow-men, and in the course of Divine Providence, seems well-nigh shipwrecked, we must remember that they were taken unawares, and without the preparation which could fit them to struggle with these tempestuous elements. In times like these the faith is the man; and they to whom it is given in larger measure owe a special duty to those who for want of it are faint at heart, uncertain in speech, feeble in effort, and purposeless in aim.

Assuming without argument a few simple propositions,—that self-government is the natural condition of an adult society, as distinguished from the immature state, in which the temporary arrangements of monarchy and oligarchy are tolerated as conveniences; that the end of all social compacts is, or ought to be, to give every child born into the world the fairest chance to make the most and the best of itself that laws can give it; that Liberty, the one of the two claimants who swears that her babe shall not be split in halves and divided between them, is the true mother of this blessed Union; that the contest in which we are engaged is one of principles overlaid by circumstances; that the longer we fight, and the more we study the movements of events and ideas, the more clearly we find the moral nature of the cause at issue emerging in the field and in the study; that all honest persons with average natural sensibility, with respectable understanding, educated in the school of northern teaching, will have eventually to range themselves in the armed or unarmed host which fights or pleads for freedom, as against every form of tyranny; if not in the front rank now, then in the rear rank by and by;—assuming these propositions, as many, perhaps most of us, are ready to do, and believing that the more they are debated before the public the more they will gain converts, we owe it to the timid and the doubting to keep the great questions of the time in unceasing and untiring agitation. They must be discussed, in all ways consistent with the public welfare, by different classes of thinkers; by priests and laymen; by statesmen and simple voters; by moralists and lawyers; by men of science and uneducated hand-laborers; by men of facts and figures, and by men of theories and aspirations; in the abstract and in the concrete; discussed and rediscussed every month, every week, every day, and almost every hour, as the telegraph tells us of some new upheaval or subsidence of the rocky base of our political order.

Such discussions may not be necessary to strengthen the convictions of the great body of loyal citizens. They may do nothing toward changing the views of those, if such there be, as some profess to believe, who follow politics as a trade. They may have no hold upon that class of persons who are defective in moral sensibility, just as other persons are wanting in an ear for music. But for the honest, vacillating minds, the tender consciences supported by the tremulous knees of an infirm intelligence, the timid compromisers who are always trying to curve the straight lines and round the sharp angles of eternal law, the continual debate of these living questions is the one offered means of grace and hope of earthly redemption. And thus a true, unhesitating patriot may be willing to listen with patience to arguments which he does not need, to appeals which have no special significance for him, in the hope that some less clear in mind or less courageous in temper may profit by them.

As we look at the condition in which we find ourselves on this fourth day of July, 1863, at the beginning of the Eighty-eighth Year of American Independence, we may well ask ourselves what right we have to indulge in public rejoicings. If the war in which we are engaged is an accidental one, which might have been avoided but for our fault; if it is for any ambitious or unworthy purpose on our part; if it is hopeless, and we are madly persisting in it; if it is our duty and in our power to make a safe and honorable peace, and we refuse to do it; if our free institutions are in danger of becoming subverted, and giving place to an irresponsible tyranny; if we are moving in the narrow circles which are to ingulf us in national ruin,—then we had better sing a dirge, and leave this idle assemblage, and hush the noisy cannon which are reverberating through the air, and tear down the scaffolds which are soon to blaze with fiery symbols; for it is mourning and not joy that should cover the land; there should be silence, and not the echo of noisy gladness, in our streets; and the emblems with which we tell our nation's story and prefigure its future should be traced, not in fire, but in ashes.

If, on the other hand, this war is no accident, but an inevitable result of long incubating causes; inevitable as the cataclysms that swept away the monstrous births of primeval nature; if it is for no mean, unworthy end, but for national life, for liberty everywhere, for humanity, for the kingdom of God on earth; if it is not hopeless, but only growing to such dimensions that the world shall remember the final triumph of right throughout all time; if there is no safe and honorable peace for us but a peace proclaimed from the capital of every revolted province in the name of the sacred, inviolable Union; if the fear of tyranny is a phantasm, conjured up by the imagination of the weak, acted on by the craft of the cunning; if so far from circling inward to the gulf of our perdition, the movement of past years is reversed, and every revolution carries us farther and farther from the centre of the vortex, until, by God's blessing, we shall soon find ourselves freed from the outermost coil of the accursed spiral; if all these things are true; if we may hope to make them seem true, or even probable, to the doubting soul, in an hour's discourse, then we may join without madness in the day's exultant festivities; the bells may ring, the cannon may roar, the incense of our harmless saltpetre fill the air, and the children who are to inherit the fruit of these toiling, agonizing years, go about unblamed, making day and night vocal with their jubilant patriotism.

The struggle in which we are engaged was inevitable; it might have come a little sooner, or a little later, but it must have come. The disease of the nation was organic, and not functional, and the rough chirurgery of war was its only remedy.

In opposition to this view, there are many languid thinkers who lapse into a forlorn belief that if this or that man had never lived, or if this or that other man had not ceased to live, the country might have gone on in peace and prosperity, until its felicity merged in the glories of the millennium. If Mr. Calhoun had never proclaimed his heresies; if Mr. Garrison had never published his paper; if Mr. Phillips, the Cassandra in masculine shape of our long prosperous Ilium, had never uttered his melodious prophecies; if the silver tones of Mr. Clay had still sounded in the senate-chamber to smooth the billows of contention; if the Olympian brow of Daniel Webster had been lifted from the dust to fix its awful frown on the darkening scowl of rebellion,—we might have been spared this dread season of convulsion. All this is but simple Martha's faith, without the reason she could have given: "If Thou hadst been here, my brother had not died."

They little know the tidal movements of national thought and feeling, who believe that they depend for existence on a few swimmers who ride their waves. It is not Leviathan that leads the ocean from continent to continent, but the ocean which bears his mighty bulk as it wafts its own bubbles. If this is true of all the narrower manifestations of human progress, how much more must it be true of those broad movements in the intellectual and spiritual domain which interest all mankind? But in the more limited ranges referred to, no fact is more familiar than that there is a simultaneous impulse acting on many individual minds at once, so that genius comes in clusters, and shines rarely as a single star. You may trace a common motive and force in the pyramid-builders of the earliest recorded antiquity, in the evolution of Greek architecture, and in the sudden springing up of those wondrous cathedrals of the twelfth and following centuries, growing out of the soil with stem and bud and blossom, like flowers of stone whose seeds might well have been the flaming aerolites cast over the battlements of heaven. You may see the same law showing itself in the brief periods of glory which make the names of Pericles and Augustus illustrious with reflected splendors; in the painters, the sculptors, the scholars of "Leo's golden days"; in the authors of the Elizabethan time; in the poets of the first part of this century following that dreary period, suffering alike from the silence of Cowper and the song of Hayley. You may accept the fact as natural, that Zwingli and Luther, without knowing each other, preached the same reformed gospel; that Newton, and Hooke, and Halley, and Wren arrived independently of each other at the great law of the diminution of gravity with the square of the distance; that Leverrier and Adams felt their hands meeting, as it were, as they stretched them into the outer darkness beyond the orbit of Uranus, in search of the dim, unseen Planet; that Fulton and Bell, that Wheatstone and Morse, that Daguerre and Niepce, were moving almost simultaneously in parallel paths to the same end. You see why Patrick Henry, in Richmond, and Samuel Adams, in Boston, were startling the crown officials with the same accents of liberty, and why the Mecklenburg Resolutions had the very ring of the Protest of the Province of Massachusetts. This law of simultaneous intellectual movement, recognized by all thinkers, expatiated upon by Lord Macaulay and by Mr. Herbert Spencer among recent writers, is eminently applicable to that change of thought and feeling which necessarily led to the present conflict.

The antagonism of the two sections of the Union was not the work of this or that enthusiast or fanatic. It was the consequence of a movement in mass of two different forms of civilization in different directions, and the men to whom it was attributed were only those who represented it most completely, or who talked longest and loudest about it. Long before the accents of those famous statesmen referred to ever resounded in the halls of the Capitol, long before the "Liberator" opened its batteries, the controversy now working itself out by trial of battle was foreseen and predicted. Washington warned his countrymen of the danger of sectional divisions, well knowing the line of cleavage that ran through the seemingly solid fabric. Jefferson foreshadowed the judgment to fall upon the land for its sins against a just God. Andrew Jackson announced a quarter of a century beforehand that the next pretext of revolution would be slavery. De Tocqueville recognized with that penetrating insight which analyzed our institutions and conditions so keenly, that the Union was to be endangered by slavery, not through its interests, but through the change of character it was bringing about in the people of the two sections, the same fatal change which George Mason, more than half a century before, had declared to be the most pernicious effect of the system, adding the solemn warning, now fearfully justifying itself in the sight of his descendants, that "by an inevitable chain of causes and effects, Providence punishes national sins by national calamities." The Virginian romancer pictured the far-off scenes of the conflict which he saw approaching as the prophets of Israel painted the coming woes of Jerusalem, and the strong iconoclast of Boston announced the very year when the curtain should rise on the yet unopened drama.

The wise men of the past, and the shrewd men of our own time, who warned us of the calamities in store for our nation, never doubted what was the cause which was to produce first alienation and finally rupture. The descendants of the men "daily exercised in tyranny," the "petty tyrants" as their own leading statesmen called them long ago, came at length to love the institution which their fathers had condemned while they tolerated. It is the fearful realization of that vision of the poet where the lost angels snuff up with eager nostrils the sulphurous emanations of the bottomless abyss,—so have their natures become changed by long breathing the atmosphere of the realm of darkness.

At last, in the fulness of time, the fruits of sin ripened in a sudden harvest of crime. Violence stalked into the senate-chamber, theft and perjury wound their way into the cabinet, and, finally, openly organized conspiracy, with force and arms, made burglarious entrance into a chief stronghold of the Union. That the principle which underlay these acts of fraud and violence should be irrevocably recorded with every needed sanction, it pleased God to select a chief ruler of the false government to be its Messiah to the listening world. As with Pharaoh, the Lord hardened his heart, while he opened his mouth, as of old he opened that of the unwise animal ridden by cursing Balaam. Then spake Mr. "Vice-President" Stephens those memorable words which fixed forever the theory of the new social order. He first lifted a degraded barbarism to the dignity of a philosophic system. He first proclaimed the gospel of eternal tyranny as the new revelation which Providence had reserved for the western Palestine. Hear, O heavens! and give ear, O earth! The corner-stone of the new-born dispensation is the recognized inequality of races; not that the strong may protect the weak, as men protect women and children, but that the strong may claim the authority of Nature and of God to buy, to sell, to scourge, to hunt, to cheat out of the reward of his labor, to keep in perpetual ignorance, to blast with hereditary curses throughout all time, the bronzed foundling of the New World, upon whose darkness has dawned the star of the occidental Bethlehem!

After two years of war have consolidated the opinion of the Slave States, we read in the "Richmond Examiner": "The establishment of the Confederacy is verily a distinct reaction against the whole course of the mistaken civilization of the age. For 'Liberty, Equality, Fraternity,' we have deliberately substituted Slavery, Subordination, and Government."

A simple diagram, within the reach of all, shows how idle it is to look for any other cause than slavery as having any material agency in dividing the country. Match the two broken pieces of the Union, and you will find the fissure that separates them zigzagging itself half across the continent like an isothermal line, shooting its splintery projections, and opening its reentering angles, not merely according to the limitations of particular States, but as a county or other limited section of ground belongs to freedom or to slavery. Add to this the official statement made in 1862, that "there is not one regiment or battalion, or even company of men, which was organized in or derived from the Free States or Territories, anywhere, against the Union"; throw in gratuitously Mr. Stephens's explicit declaration in the speech referred to, and we will consider the evidence closed for the present on this count of the indictment.

In the face of these predictions, these declarations, this line of fracture, this precise statement, testimony from so many sources, extending through several generations, as to the necessary effect of slavery, a priori, and its actual influence as shown by the facts, few will suppose that anything we could have done would have stayed its course or prevented it from working out its legitimate effects on the white subjects of its corrupting dominion. Northern acquiescence or even sympathy may have sometimes helped to make it sit more easily on the consciences of its supporters. Many profess to think that Northern fanaticism, as they call it, acted like a mordant in fixing the black dye of slavery in regions which would but for that have washed themselves free of its stain in tears of penitence. It is a delusion and a snare to trust in any such false and flimsy reasons where there is enough and more than enough in the institution itself to account for its growth. Slavery gratifies at once the love of power, the love of money, and the love of ease; it finds a victim for anger who cannot smite back his oppressor; and it offers to all, without measure, the seductive privileges which the Mormon gospel reserves for the true believers on earth, and the Bible of Mahomet only dares promise to the saints in heaven.

Still it is common, common even to vulgarism, to hear the remark that the same gallows-tree ought to bear as its fruit the arch-traitor and the leading champion of aggressive liberty. The mob of Jerusalem was not satisfied with its two crucified thieves; it must have a cross also for the reforming Galilean, who interfered so rudely with its conservative traditions! It is asserted that the fault was quite as much on our side as on the other; that our agitators and abolishers kindled the flame for which the combustibles were all ready on the other side of the border. If these men could have been silenced, our brothers had not died.

Who are the persons that use this argument? They are the very ones who are at the present moment most zealous in maintaining the right of free discussion. At a time when every power the nation can summon is needed to ward off the blows aimed at its life, and turn their force upon its foes,—when a false traitor at home may lose us a battle by a word, and a lying newspaper may demoralize an army by its daily or weekly stillicidium of poison, they insist with loud acclaim upon the liberty of speech and of the press; liberty, nay license, to deal with government, with leaders, with every measure, however urgent, in any terms they choose, to traduce the officer before his own soldiers, and assail the only men who have any claim at all to rule over the country, as the very ones who are least worthy to be obeyed. If these opposition members of society are to have their way now, they cannot find fault with those persons who spoke their minds freely in the past on that great question which, as we have agreed, underlies all our present dissensions.

It is easy to understand the bitterness which is often shown towards reformers. They are never general favorites. They are apt to interfere with vested rights and time-hallowed interests. They often wear an unlovely, forbidding aspect. Their office corresponds to that of Nature's sanitary commission for the removal of material nuisances. It is not the butterfly, but the beetle, which she employs for this duty. It is not the bird of paradise and the nightingale, but the fowl of dark plumage and unmelodious voice, to which is entrusted the sacred duty of eliminating the substances that infect the air. And the force of obvious analogy teaches us not to expect all the qualities which please the general taste in those whose instincts lead them to attack the moral nuisances which poison the atmosphere of society. But whether they please us in all their aspects or not, is not the question. Like them or not, they must and will perform their office, and we cannot stop them. They may be unwise, violent, abusive, extravagant, impracticable, but they are alive, at any rate, and it is their business to remove abuses as soon as they are dead, and often to help them to die. To quarrel with them because they are beetles, and not butterflies, is natural, but far from profitable. They grow none the less vigorously for being trodden upon, like those tough weeds that love to nestle between the stones of court-yard pavements. If you strike at one of their heads with the bludgeon of the law, or of violence, it flies open like the seedcapsule of a snap-weed, and fills the whole region with seminal thoughts which will spring up in a crop just like the original martyr. They chased one of these enthusiasts, who attacked slavery, from St. Louis, and shot him at Alton in 1837; and on the 23d of June just passed, the Governor of Missouri, chairman of the Committee on Emancipation, introduced to the Convention an Ordinance for the final extinction of Slavery! They hunted another through the streets of a great Northern city in 1835; and within a few weeks a regiment of colored soldiers, many of them bearing the marks of the slave-driver's whip on their backs, marched out before a vast multitude tremulous with newly-stirred sympathies, through the streets of the same city, to fight our battles in the name of God and Liberty!

The same persons who abuse the reformers, and lay all our troubles at their door, are apt to be severe also on what they contemptuously emphasize as "sentiments" considered as motives of action. It is charitable to believe that they do not seriously contemplate or truly understand the meaning of the words they use, but rather play with them, as certain so-called "learned" quadrupeds play with the printed characters set before them. In all questions involving duty, we act from sentiments. Religion springs from them, the family order rests upon them, and in every community each act involving a relation between any two of its members implies the recognition or the denial of a sentiment. It is true that men often forget them or act against their bidding in the keen competition of business and politics. But God has not left the hard intellect of man to work out its devices without the constant presence of beings with gentler and purer instincts. The breast of woman is the ever-rocking cradle of the pure and holy sentiments which will sooner or later steal their way into the mind of her sterner companion; which will by and by emerge in the thoughts of the world's teachers, and at last thunder forth in the edicts of its law-givers and masters. Woman herself borrows half her tenderness from the sweet influences of maternity; and childhood, that weeps at the story of suffering, that shudders at the picture of wrong, brings down its inspiration "from God, who is our home." To quarrel, then, with the class of minds that instinctively attack abuses, is not only profitless but senseless; to sneer at the sentiments which are the springs of all just and virtuous actions, is merely a display of unthinking levity, or of want of the natural sensibilities.

With the hereditary character of the Southern people moving in one direction, and the awakened conscience of the North stirring in the other, the open conflict of opinion was inevitable, and equally inevitable its appearance in the field of national politics. For what is meant by self-government is, that a man shall make his convictions of what is right and expedient regulate the community so far as his fractional share of the government extends. If one has come to the conclusion, be it right or wrong, that any particular institution or statute is a violation of the sovereign law of God, it is to be expected that he will choose to be represented by those who share his belief, and who will in their wider sphere do all they legitimately can to get rid of the wrong in which they find themselves and their constituents involved. To prevent opinion from organizing itself under political forms may be very desirable, but it is not according to the theory or practice of self-government. And if at last organized opinions become arrayed in hostile shape against each other, we shall find that a just war is only the last inevitable link in a chain of closely connected impulses of which the original source is in Him who gave to tender and humble and uncorrupted souls the sense of right and wrong, which, after passing through various forms, has found its final expression in the use of material force. Behind the bayonet is the law-giver's statute, behind the statute the thinker's argument, behind the argument is the tender conscientiousness of woman, woman, the wife, the mother,— who looks upon the face of God himself reflected in the unsullied soul of infancy. "Out of the mouths of babes and sucklings hast thou ordained strength, because of thine enemies."

The simplest course for the malcontent is to find fault with the order of Nature and the Being who established it. Unless the law of moral progress were changed, or the Governor of the Universe were dethroned, it would be impossible to prevent a great uprising of the human conscience against a system, the legislation relating to which, in the words of so calm an observer as De Tocqueville, the Montesquieu of our laws, presents "such unparalleled atrocities as to show that the laws of humanity have been totally perverted." Until the infinite selfishness of the powers that hate and fear the principles of free government swallowed up their convenient virtues, that system was hissed at by all the old-world civilization. While in one section of our land the attempt has been going on to lift it out of the category of tolerated wrongs into the sphere of the world's beneficent agencies, it was to be expected that the protest of Northern manhood and womanhood would grow louder and stronger until the conflict of principles led to the conflict of forces. The moral uprising of the North came with the logical precision of destiny; the rage of the "petty tyrants" was inevitable; the plot to erect a slave empire followed with fated certainty; and the only question left for us of the North was, whether we should suffer the cause of the Nation to go by default, or maintain its existence by the argument of cannon and musket, of bayonet and sabre.

The war in which we are engaged is for no meanly ambitious or unworthy purpose. It was primarily, and is to this moment, for the preservation of our national existence. The first direct movement towards it was a civil request on the part of certain Southern persons, that the Nation would commit suicide, without making any unnecessary trouble about it. It was answered, with sentiments of the highest consideration, that there were constitutional and other objections to the Nation's laying violent hands upon itself. It was then requested, in a somewhat peremptory tone, that the Nation would be so obliging as to abstain from food until the natural consequences of that proceeding should manifest themselves. All this was done as between a single State and an isolated fortress; but it was not South Carolina and Fort Sumter that were talking; it was a vast conspiracy uttering its menace to a mighty nation; the whole menagerie of treason was pacing its cages, ready to spring as soon as the doors were opened; and all that the tigers of rebellion wanted to kindle their wild natures to frenzy, was the sight of flowing blood.

As if to show how coldly and calmly all this had been calculated beforehand by the conspirators, to make sure that no absence of malice aforethought should degrade the grand malignity of settled purpose into the trivial effervescence of transient passion, the torch which was literally to launch the first missile, figuratively, to "fire the southern heart" and light the flame of civil war, was given into the trembling hand of an old white-headed man, the wretched incendiary whom history will handcuff in eternal infamy with the temple-burner of ancient Ephesus. The first gun that spat its iron insult at Fort Sumter, smote every loyal American full in the face. As when the foul witch used to torture her miniature image, the person it represented suffered all that she inflicted on his waxen counterpart, so every buffet that fell on the smoking fortress was felt by the sovereign nation of which that was the representative. Robbery could go no farther, for every loyal man of the North was despoiled in that single act as much as if a footpad had laid hands upon him to take from him his father's staff and his mother's Bible. Insult could go no farther, for over those battered walls waved the precious symbol of all we most value in the past and most hope for in the future, — the banner under which we became a nation, and which, next to the cross of the Redeemer, is the dearest object of love and honor to all who toil or march or sail beneath its waving folds of glory.

Let us pause for a moment to consider what might have been the course of events if under the influence of fear, or of what some would name humanity, or of conscientious scruples to enter upon what a few please themselves and their rebel friends by calling a "wicked war"; if under any or all these influences we had taken the insult and the violence of South Carolina without accepting it as the first blow of a mortal combat, in which we must either die or give the last and finishing stroke.

By the same title which South Carolina asserted to Fort Sumter, Florida would have challenged as her own the Gibraltar of the Gulf, and Virginia the Ehrenbreitstein of the Chesapeake. Half our navy would have anchored under the guns of these suddenly alienated fortresses, with the flag of the rebellion flying at their peaks. "Old Ironsides" herself would have perhaps sailed out of Annapolis harbor to have a wooden Jefferson Davis shaped for her figure-head at Norfolk, — for Andrew Jackson was a hater of secession, and his was no fitting effigy for the battle-ship of the red-handed conspiracy. With all the great fortresses, with half the ships and warlike material, in addition to all that was already stolen, in the traitors' hands, what chance would the loyal men in the Border States have stood against the rush of the desperate fanatics of the now triumphant faction? Where would Maryland, Kentucky, Missouri, Tennessee,—saved, or looking to be saved, even as it is, as by fire,—have been in the day of trial? Into whose hands would the Capital, the archives, the glory, the name, the very life of the nation as a nation, have fallen, endangered as all of them were, in spite of the volcanic outburst of the startled North which answered the roar of the first gun at Sumter? Worse than all, are we permitted to doubt that in the very bosom of the North itself there was a serpent, coiled but not sleeping, which only listened for the first word that made it safe to strike, to bury its fangs in the heart of Freedom, and blend its golden scales in close embrace with the deadly reptile of the cotton-fields. Who would not wish that he were wrong in such a suspicion? yet who can forget the mysterious warnings that the allies of the rebels were to be found far north of the fatal boundary line; and that it was in their own streets, against their own brothers, that the champions of liberty were to defend her sacred heritage?

Not to have fought, then, after the supreme indignity and outrage we had suffered, would have been to provoke every further wrong, and to furnish the means for its commission. It would have been to placard ourselves on the walls of the shattered fort, as the spiritless race the proud labor-thieves called us. It would have been to die as a nation of freemen, and to have given all we had left of our rights into the hands of alien tyrants in league with home-bred traitors.

Not to have fought would have been to be false to liberty everywhere, and to humanity. You have only to see who are our friends and who are our enemies in this struggle, to decide for what principles we are combating. We know too well that the British aristocracy is not with us. We know what the West End of London wishes may be result of this controversy. The two halves of this Union are the two blades of the shears, threatening as those of Atropos herself, which will sooner or later cut into shreds the old charters of tyranny. How they would exult if they could but break the rivet that makes of the two blades one resistless weapon! The man who of all living Americans had the best opportunity of knowing how the fact stood, wrote these words in March, 1862: "That Great Britain did, in the most terrible moment of our domestic trial in struggling with a monstrous social evil she had earnestly professed to abhor, coldly and at once assume our inability to master it, and then become the only foreign nation steadily contributing in every indirect way possible to verify its pre-judgment, will probably be the verdict made up against her by posterity, on a calm comparison of the evidence."

So speaks the wise, tranquil statesman who represents the nation at the Court of St. James, in the midst of embarrassments perhaps not less than those which vexed his illustrious grandfather, when he occupied the same position as the Envoy of the hated, newborn Republic.

"It cannot be denied,"—says another observer, placed on one of our national watch-towers in a foreign capital,—"it cannot be denied that the tendency of European public opinion, as delivered from high places, is more and more unfriendly to our cause"; "but the people," he adds, "everywhere sympathize with us, for they know that our cause is that of free institutions,—that our struggle is that of the people against an oligarchy." These are the words of the Minister to Austria, whose generous sympathies with popular liberty no homage paid to his genius by the class whose admiring welcome is most seductive to scholars has ever spoiled; our fellow-citizen, the historian of a great Republic which infused a portion of its life into our own,—John Lothrop Motley.

It is a bitter commentary on the effects of European, and especially of British institutions, that such men should have to speak in such terms of the manner in which our struggle has been regarded. We had, no doubt, very generally reckoned on the sympathy of England, at least, in a strife which, whatever pretexts were alleged as its cause, arrayed upon one side the supporters of an institution she was supposed to hate in earnest, and on the other its assailants. We had forgotten what her own poet, one of the truest and purest of her children, had said of his countrymen, in words which might well have been spoken by the British Premier to the American Ambassador asking for some evidence of kind feeling on the part of his government:

> *"Alas I expect it not. We found no bait*
>
> *To tempt us in thy country. Doing good,*
>
> *Disinterested good, is not our trade."*

We know full well by this time what truth there is in these honest lines. We have found out, too, who our European enemies are, and why they are our enemies. Three bending statues bear up that gilded seat, which, in spite of the time-hallowed usurpations and consecrated wrongs so long associated with its history, is still venerated as the throne. One of these supports is the pensioned church; the second is the purchased army; the third is the long-suffering people. Whenever the third caryatid comes to life and walks from beneath its burden, the capitals of Europe will be filled with the broken furniture of palaces. No wonder that our ministers find the privileged orders willing to see the ominous republic split into two antagonistic forces, each paralyzing the other, and standing in their mighty impotence a spectacle to courts and kings; to be pointed at as helots who drank themselves blind and giddy out of that broken chalice which held the poisonous draught of liberty!

We know our enemies, and they are the enemies of popular rights. We know our friends, and they are the foremost champions of political and social progress. The eloquent voice and the busy pen of John Bright have both been ours, heartily, nobly, from the first; the man of the people has been true to the cause of the people. That deep and generous thinker, who, more than any of her philosophical writers, represents the higher thought of England, John Stuart Mill, has spoken for us in tones to which none but her sordid hucksters and her selfish land-graspers can refuse to listen. Count Gasparin and Laboulaye have sent us back the echo from liberal France; France, the country of ideas, whose earlier inspirations embodied themselves for us in the person of the youthful Lafayette. Italy,—would you know on which side the rights of the people and the hopes of the future are to be found in this momentous conflict, what surer test, what ampler demonstration can you ask—than the eager sympathy of the Italian patriot whose name is the hope of the toiling many, and the dread of their oppressors, wherever it is spoken, the heroic Garibaldi?

But even when it is granted that the war was inevitable; when it is granted that it is for no base end, but first for the life of the nation, and more and more, as the quarrel deepens, for the welfare of mankind, for knowledge as against enforced ignorance, for justice as against oppression, for that kingdom of God on earth which neither the unrighteous man nor the extortioner can hope to inherit, it may still be that the strife is hopeless, and must therefore be abandoned. Is it too much to say that whether the war is hopeless or not for the North depends chiefly on the answer to the question, whether the North has virtue and manhood enough to persevere in the contest so long as its resources hold out? But how much virtue and manhood it has can never be told until they are tried, and those who are first to doubt the prevailing existence of these qualities are not commonly themselves patterns of either. We have a right to trust that this people is virtuous and brave enough not to give up a just and necessary contest before its end is attained, or shown to be unattainable for want of material agencies. What was the end to be attained by accepting the gage of battle? It was to get the better of our assailants, and, having done so, to take exactly those steps which we should then consider necessary to our present and future safety. The more obstinate the resistance, the more completely must it be subdued. It may not even have been desirable, as Mr. Mill suggested long since, that the victory over the rebellion should have been easily and speedily won, and so have failed to develop the true meaning of the conflict, to bring out the full strength of the revolted section, and to exhaust the means which would have served it for a still more desperate future effort. We cannot complain that our task has proved too easy. We give our Southern army,—for we must remember that it is our army, after all, only in a state of mutiny,—we give our Southern army credit for excellent spirit and perseverance in the face of many disadvantages. But we have a few plain facts which show the probable course of events; the gradual but sure operation of the blockade; the steady pushing back of the boundary of rebellion, in spite of resistance at many points, or even of such aggressive inroads as that which our armies are now meeting with their long lines of bayonets,—may God grant them victory!—the progress of our arms down the Mississippi; the relative value of gold and currency at Richmond and Washington. If the index-hands of force and credit continue to move in the ratio of the past two years, where will the Confederacy be in twice or thrice that time?

Either all our statements of the relative numbers, power, and wealth of the two sections of the country signify nothing, or the resources of our opponents in men and means must be much nearer exhaustion than our own. The running sand of the hour-glass gives no warning, but runs as freely as ever when its last grains are about to fall. The merchant wears as bold a face the day before he is proclaimed a bankrupt, as he wore at the height of his fortunes. If Colonel Grierson found the Confederacy "a mere shell," so far as his equestrian excursion carried him, how can we say how soon the shell will collapse? It seems impossible that our own dissensions can produce anything more than local disturbances, like the Morristown revolt, which Washington put down at once by the aid of his faithful Massachusetts soldiers. But in a rebellious state dissension is ruin, and the violence of an explosion in a strict ratio to the pressure on every inch of the containing surface. Now we know the tremendous force which has compelled the "unanimity" of the Southern people. There are men in the ranks of the Southern army, if we can trust the evidence which reaches us, who have been recruited with packs of blood-hounds, and drilled, as it were, with halters around their necks. We know what is the bitterness of those who have escaped this bloody harvest of the remorseless conspirators; and from that we can judge of the elements of destruction incorporated with many of the seemingly solid portions of the fabric of the rebellion. The facts are necessarily few, but we can reason from the laws of human nature as to what must be the feelings of the people of the South to their Northern neighbors. It is impossible that the love of the life which they have had in common, their glorious recollections, their blended histories, their sympathies as Americans, their mingled blood, their birthright as born under the same flag and protected by it the world over, their worship of the same God, under the same outward form, at least, and in the folds of the same ecclesiastical organizations, should all be forgotten, and leave nothing but hatred and eternal alienation. Men do not change in this way, and we may be quite sure that the pretended unanimity of the South will some day or other prove to have been a part of the machinery of deception which the plotters have managed with such consummate skill. It is hardly to be doubted that in every part of the South, as in New Orleans, in Charleston, in Richmond, there are multitudes who wait for the day of deliverance, and for whom the coming of "our good friends, the enemies," as Beranger has it, will be like the advent of the angels to the prison-cells of Paul and Silas. But there is no need of depending on the aid of our white Southern friends, be they many or be they few; there is material power enough in the North, if there be the will to use it, to overrun and by degrees to recolonize the South, and it is far from impossible that some such process may be a part of the mechanism of its new birth, spreading from various centres of organization, on the plan which Nature follows when she would fill a half-finished tissue with blood-vessels or change a temporary cartilage into bone.

Suppose, however, that the prospects of the war were, we need not say absolutely hopeless,—because that is the unfounded hypothesis of those whose wish is father to their thought,—but full of discouragement. Can we make a safe and honorable peace as the quarrel now stands? As honor comes before safety, let us look at that first. We have undertaken to resent a supreme insult, and have had to bear new insults and aggressions, even to the direct menace of our national capital. The blood which our best and bravest have shed will never sink into the ground until our wrongs are righted, or the power to right them is shown to be insufficient. If we stop now, all the loss of life has been butchery; if we carry out the intention with which we first resented the outrage, the earth drinks up the blood of our martyrs, and the rose of honor blooms forever where it was shed. To accept less than indemnity for the past, so far as the wretched kingdom of the conspirators can afford it, and security for the future, would discredit us in our own eyes and in the eyes of those who hate and long to be able to despise us. But to reward the insults and the robberies we have suffered, by the surrender of our fortresses along the coast, in the national gulf, and on the banks of the national river,—and this and much more would surely be demanded of us,—would place the United Fraction of America on a level with the Peruvian guano-islands, whose ignoble but coveted soil is open to be plundered by all comers!

If we could make a peace without dishonor, could we make one that would be safe and lasting? We could have an armistice, no doubt, long enough for the flesh of our wounded men to heal and their broken bones to knit together. But could we expect a solid, substantial, enduring peace, in which the grass would have time to grow in the war-paths, and the bruised arms to rust, as the old G. R. cannon rusted in our State arsenal, sleeping with their tompions in their mouths, like so many sucking lambs? It is not the question whether the same set of soldiers would be again summoned to the field. Let us take it for granted that we have seen enough of the miseries of warfare to last us for a while, and keep us contented with militia musters and sham-fights. The question is whether we could leave our children and our children's children with any secure trust that they would not have to go through the very trials we are enduring, probably on a more extended scale and in a more aggravated form.

It may be well to look at the prospects before us, if a peace is established on the basis of Southern independence, the only peace possible, unless we choose to add ourselves to the four millions who already call the Southern whites their masters. We know what the prevailing—we do not mean universal—spirit and temper of those people have been for generations, and what they are like to be after a long and bitter warfare. We know what their tone is to the people of the North; if we do not, De Bow and Governor Hammond are schoolmasters who will teach us to our heart's content. We see how easily their social organization adapts itself to a state of warfare. They breed a superior order of men for leaders, an ignorant commonalty ready to follow them as the vassals of feudal times followed their lords; and a race of bondsmen, who, unless this war changes them from chattels to human beings, will continue to add vastly to their military strength in raising their food, in building their fortifications, in all the mechanical work of war, in fact, except, it may be, the handling of weapons. The institution proclaimed as the corner-stone of their government does violence not merely to the precepts of religion, but to many of the best human instincts, yet their fanaticism for it is as sincere as any tribe of the desert ever manifested for the faith of the Prophet of Allah. They call themselves by the same name as the Christians of the North, yet there is as much difference between their Christianity and that of Wesley or of Channing, as between creeds that in past times have vowed mutual extermination. Still we must not call them barbarians because they cherish an institution hostile to civilization. Their highest culture stands out all the more brilliantly from the dark background of ignorance against which it is seen; but it would be injustice to deny that they have always shone in political science, or that their military capacity makes them most formidable antagonists, and that, however inferior they may be to their Northern fellow-countrymen in most branches of literature and science, the social elegances and personal graces lend their outward show to the best circles among their dominant class.

Whom have we then for our neighbors, in case of separation,—our neighbors along a splintered line of fracture extending for thousands of miles,—but the Saracens of the Nineteenth Century; a fierce, intolerant, fanatical people, the males of which will be a perpetual standing army; hating us worse than the Southern Hamilcar taught his swarthy boy to hate the Romans; a people whose existence as a hostile nation on our frontier is incompatible with our peaceful development? Their wealth, the proceeds of enforced labor, multiplied by the breaking up of new cottonfields, and in due time by the reopening of the slave-trade, will go to purchase arms, to construct fortresses, to fit out navies. The old Saracens, fanatics for a religion which professed to grow by conquest, were a nation of predatory and migrating warriors. The Southern people, fanatics for a system essentially aggressive, conquering, wasting, which cannot remain stationary, but must grow by alternate appropriations of labor and of land, will come to resemble their earlier prototypes. Already, even, the insolence of their language to the people of the North is a close imitation of the style which those proud and arrogant Asiatics affected toward all the nations of Europe. What the "Christian dogs" were to the followers of Mahomet, the "accursed Yankees," the "Northern mud-sills" are to the followers of the Southern Moloch. The accomplishments which we find in their choicer circles were prefigured in the court of the chivalric Saladin, and the long train of Painim knights who rode forth to conquest under the Crescent. In all branches of culture, their heathen predecessors went far beyond them. The schools of mediaeval learning were filled with Arabian teachers. The heavens declare the glory of the Oriental astronomers, as Algorab and Aldebaran repeat their Arabic names to the students of the starry firmament. The sumptuous edifice erected by the Art of the nineteenth century, to hold the treasures of its Industry, could show nothing fairer than the court which copies the Moorish palace that crowns the summit of Granada. Yet this was the power which Charles the Hammer, striking for Christianity and civilization, had to break like a potter's vessel; these were the people whom Spain had to utterly extirpate from the land where they had ruled for centuries.

Prepare, then, if you unseal the vase which holds this dangerous Afrit of Southern nationality, for a power on your borders that will be to you what the Saracens were to Europe before the son of Pepin shattered their armies, and flung the shards and shivers of their broken strength upon the refuse heap of extinguished barbarisms. Prepare for the possible fate of Christian Spain; for a slave-market in Philadelphia; for the Alhambra of a Southern caliph on the grounds consecrated by the domestic virtues of a long line of Presidents and their exemplary families. Remember the ages of border warfare between England and Scotland, closed at last by the union of the two kingdoms. Recollect the hunting of the deer on the Cheviot hills, and all that it led to; then think of the game which the dogs will follow open-mouthed across our Southern border, and all that is like to follow which the child may rue that is unborn; think of these possibilities, or probabilities, if you will, and say whether you are ready to make a peace which will give you such a neighbor; which may betray your civilization as that of half the Peninsula was given up to the Moors; which may leave your fair border provinces to be crushed under the heel of a tyrant, as Holland was left to be trodden down by the Duke of Alva!

No! no! fellow-citizens! We must fight in this quarrel until one side or the other is exhausted. Rather than suffer all that we have poured out of our blood, all that we have lavished of our substance, to have been expended in vain, and to bequeath an unsettled question, an unfinished conflict, an unavenged insult, an unrighted wrong, a stained escutcheon, a tarnished shield, a dishonored flag, an unheroic memory to the descendants of those who have always claimed that their fathers were heroes; rather than do all this, it were hardly an American exaggeration to say, better that the last man and the last dollar should be followed by the last woman and the last dime, the last child and the last copper!

There are those who profess to fear that our government is becoming a mere irresponsible tyranny. If there are any who really believe that our present Chief Magistrate means to found a dynasty for himself and family, that a coup d'etat is in preparation by which he is to become ABRAHAM, DEI GRATIA REX,—they cannot have duly pondered his letter of June 12th, in which he unbosoms himself with the simplicity of a rustic lover called upon by an anxious parent to explain his intentions. The force of his argument is not at all injured by the homeliness of his illustrations. The American people are not much afraid that their liberties will be usurped. An army of legislators is not very likely to throw away its political privileges, and the idea of a despotism resting on an open ballot-box, is like that of Bunker Hill Monument built on the waves of Boston Harbor. We know pretty well how much of sincerity there is in the fears so clamorously expressed, and how far they are found in company with uncompromising hostility to the armed enemies of the nation. We have learned to put a true value on the services of the watch-dog who bays the moon, but does not bite the thief!

The men who are so busy holy-stoning the quarterdeck, while all hands are wanted to keep the ship afloat, can no doubt show spots upon it that would be very unsightly in fair weather. No thoroughly loyal man, however, need suffer from any arbitrary exercise of power, such as emergencies always give rise to. If any half-loyal man forgets his code of half-decencies and half-duties so far as to become obnoxious to the peremptory justice which takes the place of slower forms in all centres of conflagration, there is no sympathy for him among the soldiers who are risking their lives for us; perhaps there is even more satisfaction than when an avowed traitor is caught and punished. For of all men who are loathed by generous natures, such as fill the ranks of the armies of the Union, none are so thoroughly loathed as the men who contrive to keep just within the limits of the law, while their whole conduct provokes others to break it; whose patriotism consists in stopping an inch short of treason, and whose political morality has for its safeguard a just respect for the jailer and the hangman! The simple preventive against all possible injustice a citizen is like to suffer at the hands of a government which in its need and haste must of course commit many errors, is to take care to do nothing that will directly or indirectly help the enemy, or hinder the government in carrying on the war. When the clamor against usurpation and tyranny comes from citizens who can claim this negative merit, it may be listened to. When it comes from those who have done what they could to serve their country, it will receive the attention it deserves. Doubtless there may prove to be wrongs which demand righting, but the pretence of any plan for changing the essential principle of our self-governing system is a figment which its contrivers laugh over among themselves. Do the citizens of Harrisburg or of Philadelphia quarrel to-day about the strict legality of an executive act meant in good faith for their protection against the invader? We are all citizens of Harrisburg, all citizens of Philadelphia, in this hour of their peril, and with the enemy at work in our own harbors, we begin to understand the difference between a good and bad citizen; the man that helps and the man that hinders; the man who, while the pirate is in sight, complains that our anchor is dragging in his mud, and the man who violates the proprieties, like our brave Portland brothers, when they jumped on board the first steamer they could reach, cut her cable, and bore down on the corsair, with a habeas corpus act that lodged twenty buccaneers in Fort Preble before sunset!

We cannot, then, we cannot be circling inward to be swallowed up in the whirlpool of national destruction. If our borders are invaded, it is only as the spur that is driven into the courser's flank to rouse his slumbering mettle. If our property is taxed, it is only to teach us that liberty is worth paying for as well as fighting for. We are pouring out the most generous blood of our youth and manhood; alas! this is always the price that must be paid for the redemption of a people. What have we to complain of, whose granaries are choking with plenty, whose streets are gay with shining robes and glittering equipages, whose industry is abundant enough to reap all its overflowing harvest, yet sure of employment and of its just reward, the soil of whose mighty valleys is an inexhaustible mine of fertility, whose mountains cover up such stores of heat and power, imprisoned in their coal measures, as would warm all the inhabitants and work all the machinery of our planet for unnumbered ages, whose rocks pour out rivers of oil, whose streams run yellow over beds of golden sand,—what have we to complain of?

Have we degenerated from our English fathers, so that we cannot do and bear for our national salvation what they have done and borne over and over again for their form of government? Could England, in her wars with Napoleon, bear an income-tax of ten per cent., and must we faint under the burden of an income-tax of three per cent.? Was she content to negotiate a loan at fifty-three for the hundred, and that paid in depreciated paper, and can we talk about financial ruin with our national stocks ranging from one to eight or nine above par, and the "five-twenty" war loan eagerly taken by our own people to the amount of nearly two hundred millions, without any check to the flow of the current pressing inwards against the doors of the Treasury? Except in those portions of the country which are the immediate seat of war, or liable to be made so, and which, having the greatest interest not to become the border states of hostile nations, can best afford to suffer now, the state of prosperity and comfort is such as to astonish those who visit us from other countries. What are war taxes to a nation which, as we are assured on good authority, has more men worth a million now than it had worth ten thousand dollars at the close of the Revolution,—whose whole property is a hundred times, and whose commerce, inland and foreign, is five hundred times, what it was then? But we need not study Mr. Still's pamphlet and "Thompson's Bank-Note Reporter" to show us what we know well enough, that, so far from having occasion to tremble in fear of our impending ruin, we must rather blush for our material prosperity. For the multitudes who are unfortunate enough to be taxed for a million or more, of course we must feel deeply, at the same time suggesting that the more largely they report their incomes to the tax-gatherer, the more consolation they will find in the feeling that they have served their country. But,—let us say it plainly,—it will not hurt our people to be taught that there are other things to be cared for besides money-making and money-spending; that the time has come when manhood must assert itself by brave deeds and noble thoughts; when womanhood must assume its most sacred office, "to warn, to comfort," and, if need be, "to command," those whose services their country calls for. This Northern section of the land has become a great variety shop, of which the Atlantic cities are the long-extended counter. We have grown rich for what? To put gilt bands on coachmen's hats? To sweep the foul sidewalks with the heaviest silks which the toiling artisans of France can send us? To look through plate-glass windows, and pity the brown soldiers,—or sneer at the black ones? to reduce the speed of trotting horses a second or two below its old minimum? to color meerschaums? to flaunt in laces, and sparkle in diamonds? to dredge our maidens' hair with gold-dust? to float through life, the passive shuttlecocks of fashion, from the avenues to the beaches, and back again from the beaches to the avenues? Was it for this that the broad domain of the Western hemisphere was kept so long unvisited by civilization?—for this, that Time, the father of empires, unbound the virgin zone of this youngest of his daughters, and gave her, beautiful in the long veil of her forests, to the rude embrace of the adventurous Colonist? All this is what we see around us, now, now while we are actually fighting this great battle, and supporting this great load of indebtedness. Wait till the diamonds go back to the Jews of Amsterdam; till the plate-glass window bears the fatal announcement, For Sale or to Let; till the voice of our Miriam is obeyed, as she sings,

"Weave no more silks, ye Lyons looms!"

till the gold-dust is combed from the golden locks, and hoarded to buy bread; till the fast-driving youth smokes his clay-pipe on the platform of the horse-cars; till the music-grinders cease because none will pay them; till there are no peaches in the windows at twenty-four dollars a dozen, and no heaps of bananas and pine-apples selling at the street-corners; till the ten-flounced dress has but three flounces, and it is felony to drink champagne; wait till these changes show themselves, the signs of deeper wants, the preludes of exhaustion and bankruptcy; then let us talk of the Maelstrom;—but till then, let us not be cowards with our purses, while brave men are emptying their hearts upon the earth for us; let us not whine over our imaginary ruin, while the reversed current of circling events is carrying us farther and farther, every hour, out of the influence of the great failing which was born of our wealth, and of the deadly sin which was our fatal inheritance!

Let us take a brief general glance at the wide field of discussion we are just leaving.

On Friday, the twelfth day of the month of April, in the year of our Lord eighteen hundred and sixty-one, at half-past four of the clock in the morning, a cannon was aimed and fired by the authority of South Carolina at the wall of a fortress belonging to the United States. Its ball carried with it the hatreds, the rages of thirty years, shaped and cooled in the mould of malignant deliberation. Its wad was the charter of our national existence. Its muzzle was pointed at the stone which bore the symbol of our national sovereignty. As the echoes of its thunder died away, the telegraph clicked one word through every office of the land. That word was WAR!

War is a child that devours its nurses one after another, until it is claimed by its true parents. This war has eaten its way backward through all the technicalities of lawyers learned in the infinitesimals of ordinances and statutes; through all the casuistries of divines, experts in the differential calculus of conscience and duty; until it stands revealed to all men as the natural and inevitable conflict of two incompatible forms of civilization, one or the other of which must dominate the central zone of the continent, and eventually claim the hemisphere for its development.

We have reached the region of those broad principles and large axioms which the wise Romans, the world's lawgivers, always recognized as above all special enactments. We have come to that solid substratum acknowledged by Grotius in his great Treatise: "Necessity itself which reduces things to the mere right of Nature." The old rules which were enough for our guidance in quiet times, have become as meaningless "as moonlight on the dial of the day." We have followed precedents as long as they could guide us; now we must make precedents for the ages which are to succeed us.

If we are frightened from our object by the money we have spent, the current prices of United States stocks show that we value our nationality at only a small fraction of our wealth. If we feel that we are paying too dearly for it in the blood of our people, let us recall those grand words of Samuel Adams:

"I should advise persisting in our struggle for liberty, though it were revealed from heaven that nine hundred and ninety-nine were to perish, and only one of a thousand were to survive and retain his liberty!"

What we want now is a strong purpose; the purpose of Luther, when he said, in repeating his Pater Noster, fiat voluntas MEA,—let my will be done; though he considerately added, quia Tua,—because my will is Thine. We want the virile energy of determination which made the oath of Andrew Jackson sound so like the devotion of an ardent saint that the recording angel might have entered it unquestioned among the prayers of the faithful.

War is a grim business. Two years ago our women's fingers were busy making "Havelocks." It seemed to us then as if the Havelock made half the soldier; and now we smile to think of those days of inexperience and illusion. We know now what War means, and we cannot look its dull, dead ghastliness in the face unless we feel that there is some great and noble principle behind it. It makes little difference what we thought we were fighting for at first; we know what we are fighting for now, and what we are fighting against.

We are fighting for our existence. We say to those who would take back their several contributions to that undivided unity which we call the Nation; the bronze is cast; the statue is on its pedestal; you cannot reclaim the brass you flung into the crucible! There are rights, possessions, privileges, policies, relations, duties, acquired, retained, called into existence in virtue of the principle of absolute solidarity,—belonging to the United States as an organic whole, which cannot be divided, which none of its constituent parties can claim as its own, which perish out of its living frame when the wild forces of rebellion tear it limb from limb, and which it must defend, or confess self-government itself a failure.

We are fighting for that Constitution upon which our national existence reposes, now subjected by those who fired the scroll on which it was written from the cannon at Fort Sumter, to all those chances which the necessities of war entail upon every human arrangement, but still the venerable charter of our wide Republic.

We cannot fight for these objects without attacking the one mother cause of all the progeny of lesser antagonisms. Whether we know it or not, whether we mean it or not, we cannot help fighting against the system that has proved the source of all those miseries which the author of the Declaration of Independence trembled to anticipate. And this ought to make us willing to do and to suffer cheerfully. There were Holy Wars of old, in which it was glory enough to die, wars in which the one aim was to rescue the sepulchre of Christ from the hands of infidels. The sepulchre of Christ is not in Palestine! He rose from that burial-place more than eighteen hundred years ago. He is crucified wherever his brothers are slain without cause; he lies buried wherever man, made in his Maker's image, is entombed in ignorance lest he should learn the rights which his Divine Master gave him! This is our Holy War, and we must fight it against that great General who will bring to it all the powers with which he fought against the Almighty before he was cast down from heaven. He has retained many a cunning advocate to recruit for him; he has bribed many a smooth-tongued preacher to be his chaplain; he has engaged the sordid by their avarice, the timid by their fears, the profligate by their love of adventure, and thousands of nobler natures by motives which we can all understand; whose delusion we pity as we ought always to pity the error of those who know not what they do. Against him or for him we are all called upon to declare ourselves. There is no neutrality for any single true-born American. If any seek such a position, the stony finger of Dante's awful muse points them to their place in the antechamber of the Halls of Despair,—

We must use all the means which God has put into our hands to serve him against the enemies of civilization. We must make and keep the great river free, whatever it costs us; it is strapping up the forefoot of the wild, untamable rebellion. We must not be too nice in the choice of our agents. Non eget Mauri jaculis,—no African bayonets wanted,—was well enough while we did not yet know the might of that desperate giant we had to deal with; but Tros, Tyriusve,—white or black,—is the safer motto now; for a good soldier, like a good horse, cannot be of a bad color. The iron-skins, as well as the iron-clads, have already done us noble service, and many a mother will clasp the returning boy, many a wife will welcome back the war-worn husband, whose smile would never again have gladdened his home, but that, cold in the shallow trench of the battle-field, lies the half-buried form of the unchained bondsman whose dusky bosom sheathes the bullet which would else have claimed that darling as his country's sacrifice.

We shall have success if we truly will success, not otherwise. It may be long in coming,—Heaven only knows through what trials and humblings we may have to pass before the full strength of the nation is duly arrayed and led to victory. We must be patient, as our fathers were patient; even in our worst calamities, we must remember that defeat itself may be a gain where it costs our enemy more in relation to his strength than it costs ourselves. But if, in the inscrutable providence of the Almighty, this generation is disappointed in its lofty aspirations for the race, if we have not virtue enough to ennoble our whole people, and make it a nation of sovereigns, we shall at least hold in undying honor those who vindicated the insulted majesty of the Republic, and struck at her assailants so long as a drum-beat summoned them to the field of duty.

Citizens of Boston, sons and daughters of New England, men and women of the North, brothers and sisters in the bond of the American Union, you have among you the scarred and wasted soldiers who have shed their blood for your temporal salvation. They bore your nation's emblems bravely through the fire and smoke of the battle-field; nay, their own bodies are starred with bullet-wounds and striped with sabre-cuts, as if to mark them as belonging to their country until their dust becomes a portion of the soil which they defended. In every Northern graveyard slumber the victims of this destroying struggle. Many whom you remember playing as children amidst the clover-blossoms of our Northern fields, sleep under nameless mounds with strange Southern wild-flowers blooming over them. By those wounds of living heroes, by those graves of fallen martyrs, by the hopes of your children, and the claims of your children's children yet unborn, in the name of outraged honor, in the interest of violated sovereignty, for the life of an imperilled nation, for the sake of men everywhere and of our common humanity, for the glory of God and the advancement of his kingdom on earth, your country calls upon you to stand by her through good report and through evil report, in triumph and in defeat, until she emerges from the great war of Western civilization, Queen of the broad continent, Arbitress in the councils of earth's emancipated peoples; until the flag that fell from the wall of Fort Sumter floats again inviolate, supreme, over all her ancient inheritance, every fortress, every capital, every ship, and this warring land is once more a United Nation!

CINDERS FROM THE ASHES

The personal revelations contained in my report of certain breakfast-table conversations were so charitably listened to and so good-naturedly interpreted, that I may be in danger of becoming over-communicative. Still, I should never have ventured to tell the trivial experiences here thrown together, were it not that my brief story is illuminated here and there by a glimpse of some shining figure that trod the same path with me for a time, or crossed it, leaving a momentary or lasting brightness in its track. I remember that, in furnishing a chamber some years ago, I was struck with its dull aspect as I looked round on the black-walnut chairs and bedstead and bureau. "Make me a large and handsomely wrought gilded handle to the key of that dark chest of drawers," I said to the furnisher. It was done, and that one luminous point redeemed the sombre apartment as the evening star glorifies the dusky firmament. So, my loving reader,—and to none other can such table-talk as this be addressed,—I hope there will be lustre enough in one or other of the names with which I shall gild my page to redeem the dulness of all that is merely personal in my recollections.

After leaving the school of Dame Prentiss, best remembered by infantine loves, those pretty preludes of more serious passions; by the great forfeit-basket, filled with its miscellaneous waifs and deodauds, and by the long willow stick by the aid of which the good old body, now stricken in years and unwieldy in person could stimulate the sluggish faculties or check the mischievous sallies of the child most distant from his ample chair,—a school where I think my most noted schoolmate was the present Bishop of Delaware, became the pupil of Master William Biglow. This generation is not familiar with his title to renown, although he fills three columns and a half in Mr. Duyckinck's "Cyclopaedia of American Literature." He was a humorist hardly robust enough for more than a brief local immortality. I am afraid we were an undistinguished set, for I do not remember anybody near a bishop in dignity graduating from our benches.

At about ten years of age I began going to what we always called the "Port School," because it was kept at Cambridgeport, a mile from the College. This suburb was at that time thinly inhabited, and, being much of it marshy and imperfectly reclaimed, had a dreary look as compared with the thriving

College settlement. The tenants of the many beautiful mansions that have sprung up along Main Street, Harvard Street, and Broadway can hardly recall the time when, except the "Dana House" and the "Opposition House" and the "Clark House," these roads were almost all the way bordered by pastures until we reached the "stores" of Main Street, or were abreast of that forlorn "First Row" of Harvard Street. We called the boys of that locality "Port-chucks." They called us "Cambridge-chucks," but we got along very well together in the main.

Among my schoolmates at the Port School was a young girl of singular loveliness. I once before referred to her as "the golden blonde," but did not trust myself to describe her charms. The day of her appearance in the school was almost as much a revelation to us boys as the appearance of Miranda was to Caliban. Her abounding natural curls were so full of sunshine, her skin was so delicately white, her smile and her voice were so all-subduing, that half our heads were turned. Her fascinations were everywhere confessed a few years afterwards; and when I last met her, though she said she was a grandmother, I questioned her statement, for her winning looks and ways would still have made her admired in any company.

Not far from the golden blonde were two small boys, one of them very small, perhaps the youngest boy in school, both ruddy, sturdy, quiet, reserved, sticking loyally by each other, the oldest, however, beginning to enter into social relations with us of somewhat maturer years. One of these two boys was destined to be widely known, first in literature, as author of one of the most popular books of its time and which is freighted for a long voyage; then as an eminent lawyer; a man who, if his countrymen are wise, will yet be prominent in the national councils. Richard Henry Dana, Junior, is the name he bore and bears; he found it famous, and will bequeath it a fresh renown.

Sitting on the girls' benches, conspicuous among the school-girls of unlettered origin by that look which rarely fails to betray hereditary and congenital culture, was a young person very nearly of my own age. She came with the reputation of being "smart," as we should have called it, clever as we say nowadays. This was Margaret Fuller, the only one among us who, like "Jean Paul," like "The Duke," like "Bettina," has slipped the cable of the more distinctive name to which she was anchored, and floats on the waves of speech as "Margaret." Her air to her schoolmates was marked by a certain stateliness and distance, as if she had other thoughts than theirs and was not of them. She was a great student and a great reader of what she used to call "naw-vels." I remember her so well as she appeared at school and later, that I regret that she had not been faithfully given to canvas or marble in the day of her best looks. None know her aspect who have not seen her living. Margaret, as I remember her at school and afterwards, was tall, fair complexioned, with a watery, aqua-marine lustre in her light eyes, which she used to make small, as one does who looks at the sunshine. A remarkable point about her was that long, flexile neck, arching and undulating in strange sinuous movements, which one who loved her would compare to those of a swan, and one who loved her not to those of the ophidian who tempted our common mother. Her talk was affluent, magisterial, de haut en bas, some would say euphuistic, but surpassing the talk of women in breadth and audacity. Her face kindled and reddened and dilated in every feature as she spoke, and, as I once saw her in a fine storm of indignation at the supposed ill-treatment of a relative, showed itself capable of something resembling what Milton calls the viraginian aspect.

Little incidents bear telling when they recall anything of such a celebrity as Margaret. I remember being greatly awed once, in our school-days, with the maturity of one of her expressions. Some themes were brought home from the school for examination by my father, among them one of hers. I took it up with a certain emulous interest (for I fancied at that day that I too had drawn a prize, say a five-dollar one, at least, in the great intellectual life-lottery) and read the first words.

"It is a trite remark," she began.

I stopped. Alas! I did not know what trite meant. How could I ever judge Margaret fairly after such a crushing discovery of her superiority? I doubt if I ever did; yet oh, how pleasant it would have been, at about the age, say, of threescore and ten, to rake over these ashes for cinders with her,—she in a snowy cap, and I in a decent peruke!

After being five years at the Port School, the time drew near when I was to enter college. It seemed advisable to give me a year of higher training, and for that end some public school was thought to offer advantages. Phillips Academy at Andover was well known to us. We had been up there, my father and myself, at anniversaries. Some Boston boys of well-known and distinguished parentage had been scholars there very lately, Master Edmund Quincy, Master Samuel Hurd Walley, Master Nathaniel Parker Willis,—all promising youth, who fulfilled their promise.

I do not believe there was any thought of getting a little respite of quiet by my temporary absence, but I have wondered that there was not. Exceptional boys of fourteen or fifteen make home a heaven, it is true; but I have suspected, late in life, that I was not one of the exceptional kind. I had tendencies in the direction of flageolets and octave flutes. I had a pistol and a gun, and popped at everything that stirred, pretty nearly, except the house-cat. Worse than this, I would buy a cigar and smoke it by instalments, putting it meantime in the barrel of my pistol, by a stroke of ingenuity which it gives me a grim pleasure to recall; for no maternal or other female eyes would explore the cavity of that dread implement in search of contraband commodities.

It was settled, then, that I should go to Phillips Academy, and preparations were made that I might join the school at the beginning of the autumn.

In due time I took my departure in the old carriage, a little modernized from the pattern of my Lady Bountiful's, and we jogged soberly along,—kind parents and slightly nostalgic boy,—towards the seat of learning, some twenty miles away. Up the old West Cambridge road, now North Avenue; past Davenport's tavern, with its sheltering tree and swinging sign; past the old powder-house, looking like a colossal conical ball set on end; past the old Tidd House, one of the finest of the ante-Revolutionary mansions; past Miss Swan's great square boarding-school, where the music of girlish laughter was ringing through the windy corridors; so on to Stoneham, town of the bright lake, then darkened with the recent memory of the barbarous murder done by its lonely shore; through pleasant Reading, with its oddly named village centres, "Trapelo," "Read'nwoodeend," as rustic speech had it, and the rest; through Wilmington, then renowned for its hops; so at last into the hallowed borders of the academic town.

It was a shallow, two-story white house before which we stopped, just at the entrance of the central village, the residence of a very worthy professor in the theological seminary,—learned, amiable, exemplary, but thought by certain experts to be a little questionable in the matter of homoousianism, or some such doctrine. There was a great rock that showed its round back in the narrow front yard. It looked cold and hard; but it hinted firmness and indifference to the sentiments fast struggling to get uppermost in my youthful bosom; for I was not too old for home-sickness,—who is: The carriage and my fond companions had to leave me at last. I saw it go down the declivity that sloped southward, then climb the next ascent, then sink gradually until the window in the back of it disappeared like an eye that shuts, and leaves the world dark to some widowed heart.

Sea-sickness and home-sickness are hard to deal with by any remedy but time. Mine was not a bad case, but it excited sympathy. There was an ancient, faded old lady in the house, very kindly, but very deaf, rustling about in dark autumnal foliage of silk or other murmurous fabric, somewhat given to snuff, but a very worthy gentlewoman of the poor-relation variety.

She comforted me, I well remember, but not with apples, and stayed me, but not with flagons. She went in her benevolence, and, taking a blue and white soda-powder, mingled the same in water, and encouraged me to drink the result. It might be a specific for seasickness, but it was not for home-sickness. The fiz was a mockery, and the saline refrigerant struck a colder chill to my despondent heart. I did not disgrace myself, however, and a few days cured me, as a week on the water often cures seasickness.

There was a sober-faced boy of minute dimensions in the house, who began to make some advances to me, and who, in spite of all the conditions surrounding him, turned out, on better acquaintance, to be one of the most amusing, free-spoken, mocking little imps I ever met in my life. My room-mate came later. He was the son of a clergyman in a neighboring town,—in fact I may remark that I knew a good many clergymen's sons at Andover. He and I went in harness together as well as most boys do, I suspect; and I have no grudge against him, except that once, when I was slightly indisposed, he administered to me,—with the best intentions, no doubt,—a dose of Indian pills, which effectually knocked me out of time, as Mr. Morrissey would say,—not quite into eternity, but so near it that I perfectly remember one of the good ladies told me (after I had come to my senses a little, and was just ready for a sip of cordial and a word of encouragement), with that delightful plainness of speech which so brings realities home to the imagination, that "I never should look any whiter when I was laid out as a corpse." After my room-mate and I had been separated twenty-five years, fate made us fellow-townsmen and acquaintances once more in Berkshire, and now again we are close literary neighbors; for I have just read a very pleasant article, signed by him, in the last number of the "Galaxy." Does it not sometimes seem as if we were all marching round and round in a circle, like the supernumeraries who constitute the "army" of a theatre, and that each of us meets and is met by the same and only the same people, or their doubles, twice, thrice, or a little oftener, before the curtain drops and the "army" puts off its borrowed clothes?

The old Academy building had a dreary look, with its flat face, bare and uninteresting as our own "University Building" at Cambridge, since the piazza which relieved its monotony was taken away, and, to balance the ugliness thus produced, the hideous projection was added to "Harvard Hall." Two masters sat at the end of the great room,—the principal and his assistant. Two others presided in separate rooms, one of them the late Rev. Samuel Horatio Stearns, an excellent and lovable man, who looked kindly on me, and for whom I always cherished a sincere regard, a clergyman's son, too, which privilege I did not always find the warrant of signal virtues; but no matter about that here, and I have promised myself to be amiable.

On the side of the long room was a large clock-dial, bearing these words:

YOUTH IS THE SEED-TIME OF LIFE.

I had indulged in a prejudice, up to that hour, that youth was the budding time of life, and this clock-dial, perpetually twitting me with its seedy moral, always had a forbidding look to my vernal apprehension.

I was put into a seat with an older and much bigger boy, or youth, with a fuliginous complexion, a dilating and whitening nostril, and a singularly malignant scowl. Many years afterwards he committed an act of murderous violence, and ended by going to finish his days in a madhouse. His delight was to kick my shins with all his might, under the desk, not at all as an act of hostility, but as a gratifying and harmless pastime. Finding this, so far as I was concerned, equally devoid of pleasure and profit, I managed to get a seat by another boy, the son of a very distinguished divine. He was bright enough, and more select in his choice of recreations, at least during school hours, than my late homicidal neighbor. But the principal called me up presently, and cautioned me against him as a dangerous companion. Could it be so? If the son of that boy's father could not be trusted, what boy in Christendom could? It seemed like the story of the youth doomed to be slain by a lion before reaching a certain age, and whose fate found him out in the heart of the tower where his father had shut him up for safety. Here was I, in the very dove's nest of Puritan faith, and out of one of its eggs a serpent had been hatched and was trying to nestle in my bosom! I parted from him, however, none the worse for his companionship so far as I can remember.

Of the boys who were at school with me at Andover one has acquired great distinction among the scholars of the land. One day I observed a new boy in a seat not very far from my own. He was a little fellow, as I recollect him, with black hair and very bright black eyes, when at length I got a chance to look at them. Of all the new-comers during my whole year he was the only one whom the first glance fixed in my memory, but there he is now, at this moment, just as he caught my eye on the morning of his entrance. His head was between his hands (I wonder if he does not sometimes study in that same posture nowadays!) and his eyes were fastened to his book as if he had been reading a will that made him heir to a million. I feel sure that Professor Horatio Balch Hackett will not find fault with me for writing his name under this inoffensive portrait. Thousands of faces and forms that I have known more or less familiarly have faded from my remembrance, but this presentment of the youthful student, sitting there entranced over the page of his text-book,—the child-father of the distinguished scholar that was to be,—is not a picture framed and hung up in my mind's gallery, but a fresco on its walls, there to remain so long as they hold together.

My especial intimate was a fine, rosy-faced boy, not quite so free of speech as myself, perhaps, but with qualities that promised a noble manhood, and ripened into it in due season. His name was Phinehas Barnes, and, if he is inquired after in Portland or anywhere in the State of Maine, something will be heard to his advantage from any honest and intelligent citizen of that Commonwealth who answers the question. This was one of two or three friendships that lasted. There were other friends and classmates, one of them a natural humorist of the liveliest sort, who would have been quarantined in any Puritan port, his laugh was so potently contagious.

Of the noted men of Andover the one whom I remember best was Professor Moses Stuart. His house was nearly opposite the one in which I resided and I often met him and listened to him in the chapel of the Seminary. I have seen few more striking figures in my life than his, as I remember it. Tall, lean, with strong, bold features, a keen, scholarly, accipitrine nose, thin, expressive lips, great solemnity and impressiveness of voice and manner, he was my early model of a classic orator. His air was Roman, his neck long and bare like Cicero's, and his toga,—that is his broadcloth cloak,— was carried on his arm, whatever might have been the weather, with such a statue-like rigid grace that he might have been turned into marble as he stood, and looked noble by the side of the antiques of the Vatican.

Dr. Porter was an invalid, with the prophetic handkerchief bundling his throat, and his face "festooned"—as I heard Hillard say once, speaking of one of our College professors—in folds and wrinkles. Ill health gives a certain common character to all faces, as Nature has a fixed course which she follows in dismantling a human countenance: the noblest and the fairest is but a death's-head decently covered over for the transient ceremony of life, and the drapery often falls half off before the procession has passed.

Dr. Woods looked his creed more decidedly, perhaps, than any of the Professors. He had the firm fibre of a theological athlete, and lived to be old without ever mellowing, I think, into a kind of half-heterodoxy, as old ministers of stern creed are said to do now and then,—just as old doctors grow to be sparing of the more exasperating drugs in their later days. He had manipulated the mysteries of the Infinite so long and so exhaustively, that he would have seemed more at home among the mediaeval schoolmen than amidst the working clergy of our own time.

All schools have their great men, for whose advent into life the world is waiting in dumb expectancy. In due time the world seizes upon these wondrous youth, opens the shell of their possibilities like the valves of an oyster, swallows them at a gulp, and they are for the most part heard of no more. We had two great men, grown up both of them. Which was the more awful intellectual power to be launched upon society, we debated. Time cut the knot in his rude fashion by taking one away early, and padding the other with prosperity so that his course was comparatively noiseless and ineffective. We had our societies, too; one in particular, "The Social Fraternity," the dread secrets of which I am under a lifelong obligation never to reveal. The fate of William Morgan, which the community learned not long after this time, reminds me of the danger of the ground upon which I am treading.

There were various distractions to make the time not passed in study a season of relief. One good lady, I was told, was in the habit of asking students to her house on Saturday afternoons and praying with and for them. Bodily exercise was not, however, entirely superseded by spiritual exercises, and a rudimentary form of base-ball and the heroic sport of football were followed with some spirit.

A slight immature boy finds his materials of though and enjoyment in very shallow and simple sources. Yet a kind of romance gilds for me the sober tableland of that cold New England hill where I came in contact with a world so strange to me, and destined to leave such mingled and lasting impressions. I looked across the valley to the hillside where Methuen hung suspended, and dreamed of its wooded seclusion as a village paradise. I tripped lightly down the long northern slope with facilis descensus on my lips, and toiled up again, repeating sed revocare gradum. I wandered' in the autumnal woods that crown the "Indian Ridge," much wondering at that vast embankment, which we young philosophers believed with the vulgar to be of aboriginal workmanship, not less curious, perhaps, since we call it an escar, and refer it to alluvial agencies. The little Shawshine was our swimming-school, and the great Merrimack, the right arm of four toiling cities, was within reach of a morning stroll. At home we had the small imp to make us laugh at his enormities, for he spared nothing in his talk, and was the drollest little living protest against the prevailing solemnities of the locality. It did not take much to please us, I suspect, and it is a blessing that this is apt to be so with young people. What else could have made us think it great sport to leave our warm beds in the middle of winter and "camp out,"—on the floor of our room,—with blankets disposed tent-wise, except the fact that to a boy a new discomfort in place of an old comfort is often a luxury.

More exciting occupation than any of these was to watch one of the preceptors to see if he would not drop dead while he was praying. He had a dream one night that he should, and looked upon it as a warning, and told it round very seriously, and asked the boys to come and visit him in turn, as one whom they were soon to lose. More than one boy kept his eye on him during his public devotions, possessed by the same feeling the man had who followed Van Amburgh about with the expectation, let us not say the hope, of seeing the lion bite his head off sooner or later.

Let me not forget to recall the interesting visit to Haverhill with my room-mate, and how he led me to the mighty bridge over the Merrimack which defied the ice-rafts of the river; and to the old meetinghouse, where, in its porch, I saw the door of the ancient parsonage, with the bullet-hole in it through which Benjamin Rolfe, the minister, was shot by the Indians on the 29th of August, 1708. What a vision it was when I awoke in the morning to see the fog on the river seeming as if it wrapped the towers and spires of a great city!—for such was my fancy, and whether it was a mirage of youth or a fantastic natural effect I hate to inquire too nicely.

My literary performances at Andover, if any reader who may have survived so far cares to know, included a translation from Virgil, out of which I remember this couplet, which had the inevitable cockney rhyme of beginners:

"Thus by the power of Jove's imperial arm

The boiling ocean trembled into calm."

Also a discussion with Master Phinehas Barnes on the case of Mary, Queen of Scots, which he treated argumentatively and I rhetorically and sentimentally. My sentences were praised and his conclusions adopted. Also an Essay, spoken at the great final exhibition, held in the large hall up-stairs, which hangs oddly enough from the roof, suspended by iron rods. Subject, Fancy. Treatment, brief but comprehensive, illustrating the magic power of that brilliant faculty in charming life into forgetfulness of all the ills that flesh is heir to,—the gift of Heaven to every condition and every clime, from the captive in his dungeon to the monarch on his throne; from the burning sands of the desert to the frozen icebergs of the poles, from— but I forget myself.

This was the last of my coruscations at Andover. I went from the Academy to Harvard College, and did not visit the sacred hill again for a long time.

On the last day of August, 1867, not having been at Andover, for many years, I took the cars at noon, and in an hour or a little more found myself at the station,—just at the foot of the hill. My first pilgrimage was to the old elm, which I remembered so well as standing by the tavern, and of which they used to tell the story that it held, buried in it by growth, the iron rings put round it in the old time to keep the Indians from chopping it with their tomahawks. I then began the once familiar toil of ascending the long declivity. Academic villages seem to change very slowly. Once in a hundred years the library burns down with all its books. A new edifice or two may be put up, and a new library begun in the course of the same century; but these places are poor, for the most part, and cannot afford to pull down their old barracks.

These sentimental journeys to old haunts must be made alone. The story of them must be told succinctly. It is like the opium-smoker's showing you the pipe from which he has just inhaled elysian bliss, empty of the precious extract which has given him his dream.

I did not care much for the new Academy building on my right, nor for the new library building on my left. But for these it was surprising to see how little the scene I remembered in my boyhood had changed. The Professors' houses looked just as they used to, and the stage-coach landed its passengers at the Mansion House as of old. The pale brick seminary buildings were behind me on the left, looking as if "Hollis" and "Stoughton" had been transplanted from Cambridge,—carried there in the night by orthodox angels, perhaps, like the Santa Casa. Away to my left again, but abreast of me, was the bleak, bare old Academy building; and in front of me stood unchanged the shallow oblong white house where I lived a year in the days of James Monroe and of John Quincy Adams.

The ghost of a boy was at my side as I wandered among the places he knew so well. I went to the front of the house. There was the great rock showing its broad back in the front yard. I used to crack nuts on that, whispered the small ghost. I looked in at the upper window in the farther part of the house. I looked out of that on four long changing seasons, said the ghost. I should have liked to explore farther, but, while I was looking, one came into the small garden, or what used to be the garden, in front of the house, and I desisted from my investigation and went on my way. The apparition that put me and my little ghost to flight had a dressing-gown on its person and a gun in its hand. I think it was the dressing-gown, and not the gun, which drove me off.

And now here is the shop, or store, that used to be Shipman's, after passing what I think used to be Jonathan Leavitt's bookbindery, and here is the back road that will lead me round by the old Academy building.

Could I believe my senses when I found that it was turned into a gymnasium, and heard the low thunder of ninepin balls, and the crash of tumbling pins from those precincts? The little ghost said, Never! It cannot be. But it was. "Have they a billiard-room in the upper story?" I asked myself. "Do the theological professors take a hand at all-fours or poker on weekdays, now and then, and read the secular columns of the 'Boston Recorder' on Sundays?" I was demoralized for the moment, it is plain; but now that I have recovered from the shock, I must say that the fact mentioned seems to show a great advance in common sense from the notions prevailing in my time.

I sauntered,—we, rather, my ghost and I,—until we came to a broken field where there was quarrying and digging going on,—our old base-ball ground, hard by the burial-place. There I paused; and if any thoughtful boy who loves to tread in the footsteps that another has sown with memories of the time when he was young shall follow my footsteps, I need not ask him to rest here awhile, for he will be enchained by the noble view before him. Far to the north and west the mountains of New Hampshire lifted their summits in along encircling ridge of pale blue waves. The day was clear, and every mound and peak traced its outline with perfect definition against the sky. This was a sight which had more virtue and refreshment in it than any aspect of nature that I had looked upon, I am afraid I must say for years. I have been by the seaside now and then, but the sea is constantly busy with its own affairs, running here and there, listening to what the winds have to say and getting angry with them, always indifferent, often insolent, and ready to do a mischief to those who seek its companionship. But these still, serene, unchanging mountains,—Monadnock, Kearsarge,—what memories that name recalls!—and the others, the dateless Pyramids of New England, the eternal monuments of her ancient race, around which cluster the homes of so many of her bravest and hardiest children,—I can never look at them without feeling that, vast and remote and awful as they are, there is a kind of inward heat and muffled throb in their stony cores, that brings them into a vague sort of sympathy with human hearts. It is more than a year since I have looked on those blue mountains, and they "are to me as a feeling" now, and have been ever since.

I had only to pass a wall and I was in the burial-ground. It was thinly tenanted as I remember it, but now populous with the silent immigrants of more than a whole generation. There lay the dead I had left, the two or three students of the Seminary; the son of the worthy pair in whose house I lived, for whom in those days hearts were still aching, and by whose memory the house still seemed haunted. A few upright stones were all that I recollect. But now, around them were the monuments of many of the dead whom I remembered as living. I doubt if there has been a more faithful reader of these graven stones than myself for many a long day. I listened to more than one brief sermon from preachers whom I had often heard as they thundered their doctrines down upon me from the throne-like desk. Now they spoke humbly out of the dust, from a narrower pulpit, from an older text than any they ever found in Cruden's Concordance, but there was an eloquence in their voices the listening chapel had never known. There were stately monuments and studied inscriptions, but none so beautiful, none so touching, as that which hallows the resting-place of one of the children of the very learned Professor Robinson: "Is it well with the child? And she answered, It is well."

While I was musing amidst these scenes in the mood of Hamlet, two old men, as my little ghost called them, appeared on the scene to answer to the gravedigger and his companion. They christened a mountain or two for me, "Kearnsarge" among the rest, and revived some old recollections, of which the most curious was "Basil's Cave." The story was recent, when I was there, of one Basil, or Bezill, or Buzzell, or whatever his name might have been, a member of the Academy, fabulously rich, Orientally extravagant, and of more or less lawless habits. He had commanded a cave to be secretly dug, and furnished it sumptuously, and there with his companions indulged in revelries such as the daylight of that consecrated locality had never looked upon. How much truth there was in it all I will not pretend to say, but I seem to remember stamping over every rock that sounded hollow, to question if it were not the roof of what was once Basil's Cave.

The sun was getting far past the meridian, and I sought a shelter under which to partake of the hermit fare I had brought with me. Following the slope of the hill northward behind the cemetery, I found a pleasant clump of trees grouped about some rocks, disposed so as to give a seat, a table, and a shade. I left my benediction on this pretty little natural caravansera, and a brief record on one of its white birches, hoping to visit it again on some sweet summer or autumn day.

Two scenes remained to look upon,—the Shawshine River and the Indian Ridge. The streamlet proved to have about the width with which it flowed through my memory. The young men and the boys were bathing in its shallow current, or dressing and undressing upon its banks as in the days of old; the same river, only the water changed; "The same boys, only the names and the accidents of local memory different," I whispered to my little ghost.

The Indian Ridge more than equalled what I expected of it. It is well worth a long ride to visit. The lofty wooded bank is a mile and a half in extent, with other ridges in its neighborhood, in general running nearly parallel with it, one of them still longer. These singular formations are supposed to have been built up by the eddies of conflicting currents scattering sand and gravel and stones as they swept over the continent. But I think they pleased me better when I was taught that the Indians built them; and while I thank Professor Hitchcock, I sometimes feel as if I should like to found a chair to teach the ignorance of what people do not want to know.

"Two tickets to Boston." I said to the man at the station.

But the little ghost whispered, "When you leave this place you leave me behind you."

"One ticket to Boston, if you please. Good by, little ghost."

I believe the boy-shadow still lingers around the well-remembered scenes I traversed on that day, and that, whenever I revisit them, I shall find him again as my companion.

THE PULPIT AND THE PEW

The priest is dead for the Protestant world. Luther's inkstand did not kill the devil, but it killed the priest, at least for us: He is a loss in many respects to be regretted. He kept alive the spirit of reverence. He was looked up to as possessing qualities superhuman in their nature, and so was competent to be the stay of the weak and their defence against the strong. If one end of religion is to make men happier in this world as well as in the next, mankind lost a great source of happiness when the priest was reduced to the common level of humanity, and became only a minister. Priest, which was presbyter, corresponded to senator, and was a title to respect and honor. Minister is but the diminutive of magister, and implies an obligation to render service.

It was promised to the first preachers that in proof of their divine mission they should have the power of casting out devils and talking in strange tongues; that they should handle serpents and drink poisons with impunity; that they should lay hands on the sick and they should recover. The Roman Church claims some of these powers for its clergy and its sacred objects to this day. Miracles, it is professed, are wrought by them, or through them, as in the days of the apostles. Protestantism proclaims that the age of such occurrences as the apostles witnessed is past. What does it know about miracles? It knows a great many records of miracles, but this is a different kind of knowledge.

The minister may be revered for his character, followed for his eloquence, admired for his learning, loved for his amiable qualities, but he can never be what the priest was in past ages, and is still, in the Roman Church. Dr. Arnold's definition may be found fault with, but it has a very real meaning. "The essential point in the notion of a priest is this: that he is a person made necessary to our intercourse with God, without being necessary or beneficial to us morally,—an unreasonable, immoral, spiritual necessity." He did not mean, of course, that the priest might not have all the qualities which would recommend him as a teacher or as a man, but that he had a special power, quite independent of his personal character, which could act, as it were, mechanically; that out of him went a virtue, as from the hem of his Master's raiment, to those with whom his sacred office brought him in contact.

It was a great comfort to poor helpless human beings to have a tangible personality of like nature with themselves as a mediator between them and the heavenly powers. Sympathy can do much for the sorrowing, the suffering, the dying, but to hear God himself speaking directly through human lips, to feel the touch of a hand which is the channel of communication with the unseen Omnipotent, this was and is the privilege of those who looked and those who still look up to a priesthood. It has been said, and many who have walked the hospitals or served in the dispensaries can bear witness to the truth of the assertion, that the Roman Catholics know how to die. The same thing is less confidently to be said of Protestants. How frequently is the story told of the most exemplary Protestant Christians, nay, how common is it to read in the lives of the most exemplary Protestant ministers, that they were beset with doubts and terrors in their last days! The blessing of the viaticum is unknown to them. Man is essentially an idolater,—that is, in bondage to his imagination,—for there is no more harm in the Greek word eidolon than in the Latin word imago. He wants a visible image to fix his thought, a scarabee or a crux ansata, or the modern symbols which are to our own time what these were to the ancient Egyptians. He wants a vicegerent of the Almighty to take his dying hand and bid him godspeed on his last journey. Who but such an immediate representative of the Divinity would have dared to say to the monarch just laying his head on the block, "Fils de Saint Louis, monte au ciel"?

It has been a long and gradual process to thoroughly republicanize the American Protestant descendant of the ancient priesthood. The history of the Congregationalists in New England would show us how this change has gone on, until we have seen the church become a hall open to all sorts of purposes, the pulpit come down to the level of the rostrum, and the clergyman take on the character of a popular lecturer who deals with every kind of subject, including religion.

Whatever fault we may find with many of their beliefs, we have a right to be proud of our Pilgrim and Puritan fathers among the clergy. They were ready to do and to suffer anything for their faith, and a faith which breeds heroes is better than an unbelief which leaves nothing worth being a hero for. Only let us be fair, and not defend the creed of Mohammed because it nurtured brave men and enlightened scholars, or refrain from condemning polygamy in our admiration of the indomitable spirit and perseverance of the Pilgrim Fathers of Mormonism, or justify an inhuman belief, or a cruel or foolish superstition, because it was once held or acquiesced in by men whose nobility of character we heartily recognize. The New England clergy can look back to a noble record, but the pulpit has sometimes required a homily from the pew, and may sometimes find it worth its while to listen to one even in our own days.

From the settlement of the country to the present time, the ministers have furnished the highest type of character to the people among whom they have lived. They have lost to a considerable extent the position of leaders, but if they are in our times rather to be looked upon as representatives of their congregations, they represent what is best among those of whom they are the speaking organs. We have a right to expect them to be models as well as teachers of all that makes the best citizens for this world and the next, and they have not been, and are not in these later days unworthy of their high calling. They have worked hard for small earthly compensation. They have been the most learned men the country had to show, when learning was a scarce commodity. Called by their consciences to self-denying labors, living simply, often half-supported by the toil of their own hands, they have let the light, such light as shone for them, into the minds of our communities as the settler's axe let the sunshine into their log-huts and farm-houses.

Their work has not been confined to their professional duties, as a few instances will illustrate. Often, as was just said, they toiled like day-laborers, teasing lean harvests out of their small inclosures of land, for the New England soil is not one that "laughs when tickled with a hoe," but rather one that sulks when appealed to with that persuasive implement. The father of the eminent Boston physician whose recent loss is so deeply regretted, the Reverend Pitt Clarke, forty-two years pastor of the small fold in the town of Norton, Massachusetts, was a typical example of this union of the two callings, and it would be hard to find a story of a more wholesome and useful life, within a limited and isolated circle, than that which the pious care of one of his children commemorated. Sometimes the New England minister, like worthy Mr. Ward of Stratford-on-Avon, in old England, joined the practice of medicine to the offices of his holy profession. Michael Wigglesworth, the poet of "The Day of Doom," and Charles Chauncy, the second president of Harvard College, were instances of this twofold service. In politics their influence has always been felt, and in many cases their drums ecclesiastic have beaten the reveille as vigorously, and to as good purpose, as it ever sounded in the slumbering camp. Samuel Cooper sat in council with the leaders of the Revolution in Boston. The three Northampton-born brothers Allen, Thomas, Moses, and Solomon, lifted their voices, and, when needed, their armed hands, in the cause of liberty. In later days, Elijah Parish and David Osgood carried politics into their pulpits as boldly as their antislavery successors have done in times still more recent.

The learning, the personal character, the sacredness of their office, tended, to give the New England clergy of past generations a kind of aristocratic dignity, a personal grandeur, much more felt in the days when class distinctions were recognized less unwillingly than at present. Their costume added to the effect of their bodily presence, as the old portraits illustrate for us, as those of us who remember the last of the "fair, white, curly" wigs, as it graced the imposing figure of the Reverend Dr. Marsh of Wethersfield, Connecticut, can testify. They were not only learned in the history of the past, but they were the interpreters of the prophecy, and announced coming events with a confidence equal to that with which the weather-bureau warns us of a coming storm. The numbers of the book of Daniel and the visions of the Revelation were not too hard for them. In the commonplace book of the Reverend Joel Benedict is to be found the following record, made, as it appears, about the year 1773: "Conversing with Dr. Bellamy upon the downfall of Antichrist, after many things had been said upon the subject, the Doctor began to warm, and uttered himself after this manner: 'Tell your children to tell their children that in the year 1866 something notable will happen in the church; tell them the old man says so.'"

The "old man" came pretty near hitting the mark, as we shall see if we consider what took place in the decade from 1860 to 1870. In 1864 the Pope issued the "Syllabus of Errors," which "must be considered by Romanists—as an infallible official document, and which arrays the papacy in open war against modern civilization and civil and religious freedom." The Vatican Council in 1870 declared the Pope to be the bishop of bishops, and immediately after this began the decisive movement of the party known as the "Old Catholics." In the exact year looked forward to by the New England prophet, 1866, the evacuation of Rome by the French and the publication of "Ecce Homo" appear to be the most remarkable events having Special relation to the religious world. Perhaps the National Council of the Congregationalists, held at Boston in 1865, may be reckoned as one of the occurrences which the oracle just missed.

The confidence, if not the spirit of prophecy, lasted down to a later period. "In half a century," said the venerable Dr. Porter of Conway, New Hampshire, in 1822, "there will be no Pagans, Jews, Mohammedans, Unitarians, or Methodists." The half-century has more than elapsed, and the prediction seems to stand in need of an extension, like many other prophetic utterances.

The story is told of David Osgood, the shaggy-browed old minister of Medford, that he had expressed his belief that not more than one soul in two thousand would be saved. Seeing a knot of his parishioners in debate, he asked them what they were discussing, and was told that they were questioning which of the Medford people was the elected one, the population being just two thousand, and that opinion was divided whether it would be the minister or one of his deacons. The story may or may not be literally true, but it illustrates the popular belief of those days, that the clergyman saw a good deal farther into the councils of the Almighty than his successors could claim the power of doing.

The objects about me, as I am writing, call to mind the varied accomplishments of some of the New England clergy. The face of the Revolutionary preacher, Samuel Cooper, as Copley painted it, looks upon me with the pleasantest of smiles and a liveliness of expression which makes him seem a contemporary after a hundred years' experience of eternity. The Plato on this lower shelf bears the inscription: "Ezroe Stiles, 1766. Olim e libris Rev. Jaredis Eliot de Killingworth." Both were noted scholars and philosophers. The hand-lens before me was imported, with other philosophical instruments, by the Reverend John Prince of Salem, an earlier student of science in the town since distinguished by the labors of the Essex Institute. Jeremy Belknap holds an honored place in that unpretending row of local historians. And in the pages of his "History of New Hampshire" may be found a chapter contributed in part by the most remarkable man, in many respects, among all the older clergymen preacher, lawyer, physician, astronomer, botanist, entomologist, explorer, colonist, legislator in state and national governments, and only not seated on the bench of the Supreme Court of a Territory because he declined the office when Washington offered it to him. This manifold individual was the minister of Hamilton, a pleasant little town in Essex County, Massachusetts,—the Reverend Manasseh Cutler. These reminiscences from surrounding objects came up unexpectedly, of themselves: and have a right here, as showing how wide is the range of intelligence in the clerical body thus accidentally represented in a single library making no special pretensions.

It is not so exalted a claim to make for them, but it may be added that they were often the wits and humorists of their localities. Mather Byles's facetie are among the colonial classic reminiscences. But these were, for the most part, verbal quips and quibbles. True humor is an outgrowth of character. It is never found in greater perfection than in old clergymen and old college professors. Dr. Sprague's "Annals of the American Pulpit" tells many stories of our old ministers as good as Dean Ramsay's "Scottish Reminiscences." He has not recorded the following, which is to be found in Miss Larned's excellent and most interesting History of Windham County, Connecticut. The Reverend Josiah Dwight was the minister of Woodstock, Connecticut, about the year 1700. He was not old, it is true, but he must have caught the ways of the old ministers. The "sensational" pulpit of our own time could hardly surpass him in the drollery of its expressions. A specimen or two may dispose the reader to turn over the pages which follow in a good-natured frame of mind. "If unconverted men ever got to heaven," he said, "they would feel as uneasy as a shad up the crotch of a white-oak." Some of his ministerial associates took offence at his eccentricities, and called on a visit of admonition to the offending clergyman. "Mr. Dwight received their reproofs with great meekness, frankly acknowledged his faults, and promised amendment, but, in prayer at parting, after returning thanks for the brotherly visit and admonition, 'hoped that they might so hitch their horses on earth that they should never kick in the stables of everlasting salvation.'"

It is a good thing to have some of the blood of one of these old ministers in one's veins. An English bishop proclaimed the fact before an assembly of physicians the other day that he was not ashamed to say that he had a son who was a doctor. Very kind that was in the bishop, and very proud his medical audience must have felt. Perhaps he was not ashamed of the Gospel of Luke, "the beloved physician," or even of the teachings which came from the lips of one who was a carpenter, and the son of a carpenter. So a New-Englander, even if he were a bishop, need not be ashamed to say that he consented to have an ancestor who was a minister. On the contrary, he has a right to be grateful for a probable inheritance of good instincts, a good name, and a bringing up in a library where he bumped about among books from the time when he was hardly taller than one of his father's or grandfather's folios. What are the names of ministers' sons which most readily occur to our memory as illustrating these advantages? Edward Everett, Joseph Stevens Buckminster, Ralph Waldo Emerson, George Bancroft, Richard Hildreth, James Russell Lowell, Francis Parkman, Charles Eliot Norton, were all ministers' boys. John Lothrop Motley was the grandson of the clergyman after whom he was named. George Ticknor was next door to such a descent, for his father was a deacon. This is a group which it did not take a long or a wide search to bring together.

Men such as the ministers who have been described could not fail to exercise a good deal of authority in the communities to which they belonged. The effect of the Revolution must have been to create a tendency to rebel against spiritual dictation. Republicanism levels in religion as in everything. It might have been expected, therefore, that soon after civil liberty had been established there would be conflicts between the traditional, authority of the minister and the claims of the now free and independent congregation. So it was, in fact, as for instance in the case which follows, for which the reader is indebted to Miss Lamed's book, before cited.

The ministerial veto allowed by the Saybrook Platform gave rise, in the year 1792, to a fierce conflict in the town of Pomfret, Connecticut. Zephaniah Swift, a lawyer of Windham, came out in the Windham "Herald," in all the vehemence of partisan phraseology, with all the emphasis of italics and small capitals. Was it not time, he said, for people to look about them and see whether "such despotism was founded in Scripture, in reason, in policy, or on the rights of man! A minister, by his vote, by his single voice, may negative the unanimous vote of the church! Are ministers composed of finer clay than the rest of mankind, that entitles them to this preeminence? Does a license to preach transform a man into a higher order of beings and endow him with a natural quality to govern? Are the laity an inferior order of beings, fit only to be slaves and to be governed? Is it good policy for mankind to subject themselves to such degrading vassalage and abject submission? Reason, common sense, and the Bible, with united voice, proclaim to all mankind that they are all born free and equal; that every member of a church or Christian congregation must be on the same footing in respect of church government, and that the CONSTITUTION, which delegates to one the power to negative the vote of all the rest, is SUBVERSIVE OF THE NATURAL RIGHT OF MANKIND AND REPUGNANT TO THE WORD OF GOD."

The Reverend Mr. Welch replied to the lawyer's attack, pronouncing him to be "destitute of delicacy, decency, good manners, sound judgment, honesty, manhood, and humanity; a poltroon, a cat's-paw, the infamous tool of a party, a partisan, a political weathercock, and a ragamuffin."

No Fourth-of-July orator would in our day rant like the lawyer, and no clergyman would use such language as that of the Reverend Moses Welch. The clergy have been pretty well republicanized within that last two or three generations, and are not likely to provoke quarrels by assertion of their special dignities or privileges. The public is better bred than to carry on an ecclesiastical controversy in terms which political brawlers would hardly think admissible. The minister of religion is generally treated with something more than respect; he is allowed to say undisputed what would be sharply controverted in anybody else. Bishop Gilbert Haven, of happy memory, had been discussing a religious subject with a friend who was not convinced by his arguments. "Wait till you hear me from the pulpit," he said; "there you cannot answer me." The preacher—if I may use an image which would hardly have suggested itself to him—has his hearer's head in chancery, and can administer punishment ad libitum. False facts, false reasoning, bad rhetoric, bad grammar, stale images, borrowed passages, if not borrowed sermons, are listened to without a word of comment or a look of disapprobation.

One of the ablest and most conscientiously laborious of our clergymen has lately ventured to question whether all his professional brethren invariably give utterance to their sincerest beliefs, and has been sharply criticised for so doing. The layman, who sits silent in his pew, has his rights when out of it, and among them is the right of questioning that which has been addressed to him from the privileged eminence of the pulpit, or in any way sanctioned by his religious teacher. It is nearly two hundred years since a Boston layman wrote these words: "I am not ignorant that the pious frauds of the ancient, and the inbred fire (I do not call it pride) of many of our modern divines, have precipitated them to propagate and maintain truth as well as falsehoods, in such an unfair manner as has given advantage to the enemy to suspect the whole doctrine these men have profest to be nothing but a mere trick."

So wrote Robert Calef, the Boston merchant, whose book the Reverend Increase Mather, president of Harvard College, burned publicly in the college yard. But the pity of it is that the layman had not cried out earlier and louder, and saved the community from the horror of those judicial murders for witchcraft, the blame of which was so largely attributable to the clergy.

Perhaps no, laymen have given the clergy more trouble than the doctors. The old reproach against physicians, that where there were three of them together there were two atheists, had a real significance, but not that which was intended by the sharp-tongued ecclesiastic who first uttered it. Undoubtedly there is a strong tendency in the pursuits of the medical profession to produce disbelief in that figment of tradition and diseased human imagination which has been installed in the seat of divinity by the priesthood of cruel and ignorant ages. It is impossible, or at least very difficult, for a physician who has seen the perpetual efforts of Nature— whose diary is the book he reads oftenest—to heal wounds, to expel poisons, to do the best that can be done under the given conditions,—it is very difficult for him to believe in a world where wounds cannot heal, where opiates cannot give a respite from pain, where sleep never comes with its sweet oblivion of suffering, where the art of torture is the only science cultivated, and the capacity for being tormented is the only faculty which remains to the children of that same Father who cares for the falling sparrow. The Deity has often been pictured as Moloch, and the physician has, no doubt, frequently repudiated him as a monstrosity.

On the other hand, the physician has often been renowned for piety as well as for his peculiarly professional virtue of charity,—led upward by what he sees to the source of all the daily marvels wrought before his own eyes. So it was that Galen gave utterance to that psalm of praise which the sweet singer of Israel need not have been ashamed of; and if this "heathen" could be lifted into such a strain of devotion, we need not be surprised to find so many devout Christian worshippers among the crowd of medical "atheists."

No two professions should come into such intimate and cordial relations as those to which belong the healers of the body and the headers of the mind. There can be no more fatal mistake than that which brings them into hostile attitudes with reference to each other, both having in view the welfare of their fellow-creatures. But there is a territory always liable to be differed about between them. There are patients who never tell their physician the grief which lies at the bottom of their ailments. He goes through his accustomed routine with them, and thinks he has all the elements needed for his diagnosis. But he has seen no deeper into the breast than the tongue, and got no nearer the heart than the wrist. A wise and experienced clergyman, coming to the patient's bedside,—not with the professional look on his face which suggests the undertaker and the sexton, but with a serene countenance and a sympathetic voice, with tact, with patience, waiting for the right moment,—will surprise the shy spirit into a confession of the doubt, the sorrow, the shame, the remorse, the terror which underlies all the bodily symptoms, and the unburdening of which into a loving and pitying soul is a more potent anodyne than all the drowsy sirups of the world. And, on the other hand, there are many nervous and over-sensitive natures which have been wrought up by self-torturing spiritual exercises until their best confessor would be a sagacious and wholesome-minded physician.

Suppose a person to have become so excited by religious stimulants that he is subject to what are known to the records of insanity as hallucinations: that he hears voices whispering blasphemy in his ears, and sees devils coming to meet him, and thinks he is going to be torn in pieces, or trodden into the mire. Suppose that his mental conflicts, after plunging him into the depths of despondency, at last reduce him to a state of despair, so that he now contemplates taking his own life, and debates with himself whether it shall be by knife, halter, or poison, and after much questioning is apparently making up his mind to commit suicide. Is not this a manifest case of insanity, in the form known as melancholia? Would not any prudent physician keep such a person under the eye of constant watchers, as in a dangerous state of, at least, partial mental alienation? Yet this is an exact transcript of the mental condition of Christian in "Pilgrim's Progress," and its counterpart has been found in thousands of wretched lives terminated by the act of self-destruction, which came so near taking place in the hero of the allegory. Now the wonderful book from which this example is taken is, next to the Bible and the Treatise of "De Imitatione Christi," the best-known religious work of Christendom. If Bunyan and his contemporary, Sydenham, had met in consultation over the case of Christian at the time when he was meditating self-murder, it is very possible that there might have been a difference of judgment. The physician would have one advantage in such a consultation. He would pretty certainly have received a Christian education, while the clergyman would probably know next to nothing of the laws or manifestations of mental or bodily disease. It does not seem as if any theological student was really prepared for his practical duties until he had learned something of the effects of bodily derangements, and, above all, had become familiar with the gamut of mental discord in the wards of an insane asylum.

It is a very thoughtless thing to say that the physician stands to the divine in the same light as the divine stands to the physician, so far as each may attempt to handle subjects belonging especially to the other's profession. Many physicians know a great deal more about religious matters than they do about medicine. They have read the Bible ten times as much as they ever read any medical author. They have heard scores of sermons for one medical lecture to which they have listened. They often hear much better preaching than the average minister, for he hears himself chiefly, and they hear abler men and a variety of them. They have now and then been distinguished in theology as well as in their own profession. The name of Servetus might call up unpleasant recollections, but that of another medical practitioner may be safely mentioned. "It was not till the middle of the last century that the question as to the authorship of the Pentateuch was handled with anything like a discerning criticism. The first attempt was made by a layman, whose studies we might have supposed would scarcely have led him to such an investigation." This layman was "Astruc, doctor and professor of medicine in the Royal College at Paris, and court physician to Louis XIV." The quotation is from the article "Pentateuch" in Smith's "Dictionary of the Bible," which, of course, lies on the table of the least instructed clergyman. The sacred profession has, it is true, returned the favor by giving the practitioner of medicine Bishop Berkeley's "Treatise on Tar-water," and the invaluable prescription of that "aged clergyman whose sands of life"——but let us be fair, if not generous, and remember that Cotton Mather shares with Zabdiel Boylston the credit of introducing the practice of inoculation into America. The professions should be cordial allies, but the church-going, Bible-reading physician ought to know a great deal more of the subjects included under the general name of theology than the clergyman can be expected to know of medicine. To say, as has been said not long since, that a young divinity student is as competent to deal with the latter as an old physician is to meddle with the former, suggests the idea that wisdom is not an heirloom in the family of the one who says it. What a set of idiots our clerical teachers must have been and be, if, after a quarter or half a century of their instruction, a person of fair intelligence is utterly incompetent to form any opinion about the subjects which they have been teaching, or trying to teach him, so long!

A minister must find it very hard work to preach to hearers who do not believe, or only half believe, what he preaches. But pews without heads in them are a still more depressing spectacle. He may convince the doubter and reform the profligate. But he cannot produce any change on pine and mahogany by his discourses, and the more wood he sees as he looks along his floor and galleries, the less his chance of being useful. It is natural that in times like the present changes of faith and of place of worship should be far from infrequent. It is not less natural that there should be regrets on one side and gratification on the other, when such changes occur. It even happens occasionally that the regrets become aggravated into reproaches, rarely from the side which receives the new accessions, less rarely from the one which is left. It is quite conceivable that the Roman Church, which considers itself the only true one, should look on those who leave its communion as guilty of a great offence. It is equally natural that a church which considers Pope and Pagan a pair of murderous giants, sitting at the mouths of their caves, alike in their hatred to true Christians, should regard any of its members who go over to Romanism as lost in fatal error. But within the Protestant fold there are many compartments, and it would seem that it is not a deadly defection to pass from one to another.

So far from such exchanges between sects being wrong, they ought to happen a great deal oftener than they do. All the larger bodies of Christians should be constantly exchanging members. All men are born with conservative or aggressive tendencies: they belong naturally with the idol-worshippers or the idol-breakers. Some wear their fathers' old clothes, and some will have a new suit. One class of men must have their faith hammered in like a nail, by authority; another class must have it worked in like a screw, by argument. Members of one of these classes often find themselves fixed by circumstances in the other. The late Orestes A. Brownson used to preach at one time to a little handful of persons, in a small upper room, where some of them got from him their first lesson about the substitution of reverence for idolatry, in dealing with the books they hold sacred. But after a time Mr. Brownson found he had mistaken his church, and went over to the Roman Catholic establishment, of which he became and remained to his dying day one of the most stalwart champions. Nature is prolific and ambidextrous. While this strong convert was trying to carry us back to the ancient faith, another of her sturdy children, Theodore Parker, was trying just as hard to provide a new church for the future. One was driving the sheep into the ancient fold, while the other was taking down the bars that kept them out of the new pasture. Neither of these powerful men could do the other's work, and each had to find the task for which he was destined.

The "old gospel ship," as the Methodist song calls it, carries many who would steer by the wake of their vessel. But there are many others who do not trouble themselves to look over the stern, having their eyes fixed on the light-house in the distance before them. In less figurative language, there are multitudes of persons who are perfectly contented with the old formulae of the church with which they and their fathers before them have been and are connected, for the simple reason that they fit, like old shoes, because they have been worn so long, and mingled with these, in the most conservative religious body, are here and there those who are restless in the fetters of a confession of faith to which they have pledged themselves without believing in it. This has been true of the Athanasian creed, in the Anglican Church, for two centuries more or less, unless the Archbishop of Canterbury, Tillotson, stood alone in wishing the church were well rid of it. In fact, it has happened to the present writer to hear the Thirty-nine Articles summarily disposed of by one of the most zealous members of the American branch of that communion, in a verb of one syllable, more familiar to the ears of the forecastle than to those of the vestry.

But on the other hand, it is far from uncommon to meet with persons among the so-called "liberal" denominations who are uneasy for want of a more definite ritual and a more formal organization than they find in their own body. Now, the rector or the minister must be well aware that there are such cases, and each of them must be aware that there are individuals under his guidance whom he cannot satisfy by argument, and who really belong by all their instincts to another communion. It seems as if a thoroughly honest, straight-collared clergyman would say frankly to his restless parishioner: "You do not believe the central doctrines of the church which you are in the habit of attending. You belong properly to Brother A.'s or Brother B.'s fold, and it will be more manly and probably more profitable for you to go there than to stay with us." And, again, the rolling-collared clergyman might be expected to say to this or that uneasy listener: "You are longing for a church which will settle your beliefs for you, and relieve you to a great extent from the task, to which you seem to be unequal, of working out your own salvation with fear and trembling. Go over the way to Brother C.'s or Brother D.'s; your spine is weak, and they will furnish you a back-board which will keep you straight and make you comfortable." Patients are not the property of their physicians, nor parishioners of their ministers.

As for the children of clergymen, the presumption is that they will adhere to the general belief professed by their fathers. But they do not lose their birthright or their individuality, and have the world all before them to choose their creed from, like other persons. They are sometimes called to account for attacking the dogmas they are supposed to have heard preached from their childhood. They cannot defend themselves, for various good reasons. If they did, one would have to say he got more preaching than was good for him, and came at last to feel about sermons and their doctrines as confectioners' children do about candy. Another would have to own that he got his religious belief, not from his father, but from his mother. That would account for a great deal, for the milk in a woman's veins sweetens, or at least, dilutes an acrid doctrine, as the blood of the motherly cow softens the virulence of small-pox, so that its mark survives only as the seal of immunity. Another would plead atavism, and say he got his religious instincts from his great-grandfather, as some do their complexion or their temper. Others would be compelled to confess that the belief of a wife or a sister had displaced that which they naturally inherited. No man can be expected to go thus into the details of his family history, and, therefore, it is an ill-bred and indecent thing to fling a man's father's creed in his face, as if he had broken the fifth commandment in thinking for himself in the light of a new generation. Common delicacy would prevent him from saying that he did not get his faith from his father, but from somebody else, perhaps from his grandmother Lois and his mother Eunice, like the young man whom the Apostle cautioned against total abstinence.

It is always the right, and may sometimes be the duty, of the layman to call the attention of the clergy to the short-comings and errors, not only of their own time, but also of the preceding generations, of which they are the intellectual and moral product. This is especially true when the authority of great names is fallen back upon as a defence of opinions not in themselves deserving to be upheld. It may be very important to show that the champions of this or that set of dogmas, some of which are extinct or obsolete as beliefs, while others retain their vitality, held certain general notions which vitiated their conclusions. And in proportion to the eminence of such champions, and the frequency with which their names are appealed to as a bulwark of any particular creed or set of doctrines, is it urgent to show into what obliquities or extravagances or contradictions of thought they have been betrayed.

In summing up the religious history of New England, it would be just and proper to show the agency of the Mathers, father and son, in the witchcraft delusion. It would be quite fair to plead in their behalf the common beliefs of their time. It would be an extenuation of their acts that, not many years before, the great and good magistrate, Sir Matthew Hale, had sanctioned the conviction of prisoners accused of witchcraft. To fall back on the errors of the time is very proper when we are trying our predecessors in foro conscientace: The houses they dwelt in may have had some weak or decayed beams and rafters, but they served for their shelter, at any rate. It is quite another matter when those rotten timbers are used in holding up the roofs over our own heads. Still more, if one of our ancestors built on an unsafe or an unwholesome foundation, the best thing we can do is to leave it and persuade others to leave it if we can. And if we refer to him as a precedent, it must be as a warning and not as a guide.

Such was the reason of the present writer's taking up the writings of Jonathan Edwards for examination in a recent essay. The "Edwardsian" theology is still recognized as a power in and beyond the denomination to which he belonged. One or more churches bear his name, and it is thrown into the scale of theological belief as if it added great strength to the party which claims him. That he was a man of extraordinary endowments and deep spiritual nature was not questioned, nor that he was a most acute reasoner, who could unfold a proposition into its consequences as patiently, as convincingly, as a palaeontologist extorts its confession from a fossil fragment. But it was maintained that so many dehumanizing ideas were mixed up with his conceptions of man, and so many diabolizing attributes embodied in his imagination of the Deity, that his system of beliefs was tainted throughout by them, and that the fact of his being so remarkable a logician recoiled on the premises which pointed his inexorable syllogisms to such revolting conclusions. When he presents us a God, in whose sight children, with certain not too frequent exceptions, "are young vipers, and are infinitely more hateful than vipers;" when he gives the most frightful detailed description of infinite and endless tortures which it drives men and women mad to think of prepared for "the bulk of mankind;" when he cruelly pictures a future in which parents are to sing hallelujahs of praise as they see their children driven into the furnace, where they are to lie "roasting" forever,—we have a right to say that the man who held such beliefs and indulged in such imaginations and expressions is a burden and not a support in reference to the creed with which his name is associated. What heathenism has ever approached the horrors of this conception of human destiny? It is not an abuse of language to apply to such a system of beliefs the name of Christian pessimism.

If these and similar doctrines are so generally discredited as some appear to think, we might expect to see the change showing itself in catechisms and confessions of faith, to hear the joyful news of relief from its horrors in all our churches, and no longer to read in the newspapers of ministers rejected or put on trial for heresy because they could not accept the most dreadful of these doctrines. Whether this be so or not, it must be owned that the name of Jonathan Edwards does at this day carry a certain authority with it for many persons, so that anything he believed gains for them some degree of probability from that circumstance. It would, therefore, be of much interest to know whether he was trustworthy in his theological speculations, and whether he ever changed his belief with reference to any of the great questions above alluded to.

Some of our readers may remember a story which got abroad many years ago that a certain M. Babinet, a scientific Frenchman of note, had predicted a serious accident soon to occur to the planet on which we live by the collision with it of a great comet then approaching us, or some such occurrence. There is no doubt that this prediction produced anxiety and alarm in many timid persons. It became a very interesting question with them who this M. Babinet might be. Was he a sound observer, who had made other observations and predictions which had proved accurate? Or was he one of those men who are always making blunders for other people to correct? Is he known to have changed his opinion as to the approaching disastrous event?

So long as there were any persons made anxious by this prediction, so long as there was even one who believed that he, and his family, and his nation, and his race, and the home of mankind, with all its monuments, were very soon to be smitten in mid-heaven and instantly shivered into fragments, it was very desirable to find any evidence that this prophet of evil was a man who held many extravagant and even monstrous opinions. Still more satisfactory would it be if it could be shown that he had reconsidered his predictions, and declared that he could not abide by his former alarming conclusions. And we should think very ill of any astronomer who would not rejoice for the sake of his fellow-creatures, if not for his own, to find the threatening presage invalidated in either or both of the ways just mentioned, even though he had committed himself to M. Babinet's dire belief.

But what is the trivial, temporal accident of the wiping out of a planet and its inhabitants to the infinite catastrophe which shall establish a mighty world of eternal despair? And which is it most desirable for mankind to have disproved or weakened, the grounds of the threat of M. Babinet, or those of the other infinitely more terrible comminations, so far as they rest on the authority of Jonathan Edwards?

The writer of this paper had been long engaged in the study of the writings of Edwards, with reference to the essay he had in contemplation, when, on speaking of the subject to a very distinguished orthodox divine, this gentleman mentioned the existence of a manuscript of Edwards which had been held back from the public on account of some opinions or tendencies it contained, or was suspected of containing "High Arianism" was the exact expression he used with reference to it. On relating this fact to an illustrious man of science, whose name is best known to botanists, but is justly held in great honor by the orthodox body to which he belongs, it appeared that he, too, had heard of such a manuscript, and the questionable doctrine associated with it in his memory was Sabellianism. It was of course proper in the writer of an essay on Jonathan Edwards to mention the alleged existence of such a manuscript, with reference to which the same caution seemed to have been exercised as that which led, the editor of his collected works to suppress the language Edwards had used about children.

This mention led to a friendly correspondence between the writer and one of the professors in the theological school at Andover, and finally to the publication of a brief essay, which, for some reason, had been withheld from publication for more than a century. Its title is "Observations concerning the Scripture OEconomy of the Trinity and Covenant of Redemption. By Jonathan Edwards." It contains thirty-six pages and a half, each small page having about two hundred words. The pages before the reader will be found to average about three hundred and twenty-five words. An introduction and an appendix by the editor, Professor Egbert C. Smyth, swell the contents to nearly a hundred pages, but these additions, and the circumstance that it is bound in boards, must not lead us to overlook the fact that the little volume is nothing more than a pamphlet in book's clothing.

A most extraordinary performance it certainly is, dealing with the arrangements entered into by the three persons of the Trinity, in as bald and matter-of-fact language and as commercial a spirit as if the author had been handling the adjustment of a limited partnership between three retail tradesmen. But, lest a layman's judgment might be considered insufficient, the treatise was submitted by the writer to one of the most learned of our theological experts,—the same who once informed a church dignitary, who had been attempting to define his theological position, that he was a Eutychian,—a fact which he seems to have been no more aware of than M. Jourdain was conscious that he had been speaking prose all his life. The treatise appeared to this professor anti-trinitarian, not in the direction of Unitarianism, however, but of Tritheism. Its anthropomorphism affected him like blasphemy, and the paper produced in him the sense of "great disgust," which its whole character might well excite in the unlearned reader.

All this is, however, of little importance, for this is not the work of Edwards referred to by the present writer in his previous essay. The tract recently printed as a volume may be the one referred to by Dr. Bushnell, in 1851, but of this reference by him the writer never heard until after his own essay was already printed. The manuscript of the "Observations" was received by Professor Smyth, as he tells us in his introduction, about fifteen years ago, from the late Reverend William T. Dwight, D. D., to whom it was bequeathed by his brother, the Reverend Dr. Sereno E. Dwight.

But the reference of the present writer was to another production of the great logician, thus spoken of in a quotation from "the accomplished editor of the Hartford 'Courant,'" to be found in Professor Smyth's introduction:

"It has long been a matter of private information that Professor Edwards A. Park, of Andover, had in his possession an published manuscript of Edwards of considerable extent, perhaps two thirds as long as his treatise on the will. As few have ever seen the manuscript, its contents are only known by vague reports.... It is said that it contains a departure from his published views on the Trinity and a modification of the view of original sin. One account of it says that the manuscript leans toward Sabellianism, and that it even approaches Pelagianism."

It was to this "suppressed" manuscript the present writer referred, and not to the slender brochure recently given to the public. He is bound, therefore, to say plainly that to satisfy inquirers who may be still in doubt with reference to Edwards's theological views, it would be necessary to submit this manuscript, and all manuscripts of his which have been kept private, to their inspection, in print, if possible, so that all could form their own opinion about it or them.

The whole matter may be briefly stated thus: Edwards believed in an eternity of unimaginable horrors for "the bulk of mankind." His authority counts with many in favor of that belief, which affects great numbers as the idea of ghosts affected Madame de Stall: "Je n'y crois pas, mais je les crains."

This belief is one which it is infinitely desirable to the human race should be shown to be possibly, probably, or certainly erroneous. It is, therefore, desirable in the interest of humanity that any force the argument in its favor may derive from Edwards's authority should be weakened by showing that he was capable of writing most unwisely, and if it should be proved that he changed his opinions, or ran into any "heretical" vagaries, by using these facts against the validity of his judgment. That he was capable of writing most unwisely has been sufficiently shown by the recent publication of his "Observations." Whether he, anywhere contradicted what were generally accepted as his theological opinions, or how far he may have lapsed into heresies, the public will never rest satisfied until it sees and interprets for itself everything that is open to question which may be contained in his yet unpublished manuscripts. All this is not in the least a personal affair with the writer, who, in the course of his studies of Edwards's works, accidentally heard, from the unimpeachable sources sufficiently indicated, the reports, which it seems must have been familiar to many, that there was unpublished matter bearing on the opinions of the author through whose voluminous works he had been toiling. And if he rejoiced even to hope that so wise a man as Edwards has been considered, so good a man as he is recognized to have been, had, possibly in his changes of opinion, ceased to think of children as vipers, and of parents as shouting hallelujahs while their lost darlings were being driven into the flames, where is the theologian who would not rejoice to hope so with him or who would be willing to tell his wife or his daughter that he did not?

The real, vital division of the religious part of our Protestant communities is into Christian optimists and Christian pessimists. The Christian optimist in his fullest development is characterized by a cheerful countenance, a voice in the major key, an undisguised enjoyment of earthly comforts, and a short confession of faith. His theory of the universe is progress; his idea of God is that he is a Father with all the true paternal attributes, of man that he is destined to come into harmony with the key-note of divine order, of this earth that it is a training school for a better sphere of existence. The Christian pessimist in his most typical manifestation is apt to wear a solemn aspect, to speak, especially from the pulpit, in the minor key, to undervalue the lesser enjoyments of life, to insist on a more extended list of articles of belief. His theory of the universe recognizes this corner of it as a moral ruin; his idea of the Creator is that of a ruler whose pardoning power is subject to the veto of what is called "justice;" his notion of man is that he is born a natural hater of God and goodness, and that his natural destiny is eternal misery. The line dividing these two great classes zigzags its way through the religious community, sometimes following denominational layers and cleavages, sometimes going, like a geological fracture, through many different strata. The natural antagonists of the religious pessimists are the men of science, especially the evolutionists, and the poets. It was but a conditioned prophecy, yet we cannot doubt what was in Milton's mind when he sang, in one of the divinest of his strains, that

"Hell itself will pass away,

And leave her dolorous mansions to the peering day."

And Nature, always fair if we will allow her time enough, after giving mankind the inspired tinker who painted the Christian's life as that of a hunted animal, "never long at ease," desponding, despairing, on the verge of self-murder,—painted it with an originality, a vividness, a power and a sweetness, too, that rank him with the great authors of all time,—kind Nature, after this gift, sent as his counterpoise the inspired ploughman, whose songs have done more to humanize the hard theology of Scotland than all the rationalistic sermons that were ever preached. Our own Whittier has done and is doing the same thing, in a far holier spirit than Burns, for the inherited beliefs of New England and the country to which New England belongs. Let me sweeten these closing paragraphs of an essay not meaning to hold a word of bitterness with a passage or two from the lay-preacher who is listened to by a larger congregation than any man who speaks from the pulpit. Who will not hear his words with comfort and rejoicing when he speaks of "that larger hope which, secretly cherished from the times of Origen and Duns Scotus to those of Foster and Maurice, has found its fitting utterance in the noblest poem of the age?"

It is Tennyson's "In Memoriam" to which he refers, and from which he quotes four verses, of which this is the last:

"Behold! we know not anything

I can but trust that good shall fall

At last,—far off,—at last, to all,

And every winter change to spring."

If some are disposed to think that the progress of civilization and the rapidly growing change of opinion renders unnecessary any further effort to humanize "the Gospel of dread tidings;" if any believe the doctrines of the Longer and Shorter Catechism of the Westminster divines are so far obsolete as to require no further handling; if there are any who thank these subjects have lost their interest for living souls ever since they themselves have learned to stay at home on Sundays, with their cakes and ale instead of going to meeting,—not such is Mr. Whittier's opinion, as we may infer from his recent beautiful poem, "The Minister's Daughter." It is not science alone that the old Christian pessimism has got to struggle with, but the instincts of childhood, the affections of maternity, the intuitions of poets, the contagious humanity of the philanthropist,—in short, human nature and the advance of civilization. The pulpit has long helped the world, and is still one of the chief defences against the dangers that threaten society, and it is worthy now, as it always has been in its best representation, of all love and honor. But many of its professed creeds imperatively demand revision, and the pews which call for it must be listened to, or the preacher will by and by find himself speaking to a congregation of bodiless echoes by and by find himself speaking to a congregation of bodiless echoes.

www.ingramcontent.com/pod-product-compliance
Lightning Source LLC
LaVergne TN
LVHW091550170726
843492LV00007B/2120